I0759579

THE INDONESIAN VEGETARIAN TABLE

To Nick, Chris
and Jeremy.

THE INDONESIAN VEGETARIAN TABLE

Petty Pandean-Elliott

Vegan

Dairy-free

Gluten-free

Nut-free

30 Minutes or Less

5 Ingredients or Fewer

Introduction

A Journey through the Archipelago

This book is the result of my many journeys around the communities of the Indonesian archipelago, exploring one of the world's greatest epicentres of plant-based food. Indonesia comprises a vast land of over 17,000 islands, and the country's tropical climate and fertile volcanic soils offer a simply incredible choice of edible plants. I hope that by combining insights into our history and ancient agricultural practice, I can provide you with an entertaining and informative introduction to the distinctive and flavourful culinary heritage of my home. As the world faces climate change and food insecurity, this book offers not just a glimpse into our culinary past but a quiet vision of a future nourished by local roots and sustainable ways of living.

Sensory Moments

Indonesian vegetarian food is a full sensory experience – one that engages not just taste and smell but also touch, sight and memory. The aroma of *woku*, a spice and herb blend from Manado, North Sulawesi, immediately takes me back home. It's made with turmeric, lemongrass, makrut lime leaves, ginger, galangal, chillies, shallots and garlic, sizzling in a hot wok until the fragrance fills the kitchen. There's the sharp, fresh scent of Dabu-Dabu (page 34), a spicy tomato salsa, and the comforting sweetness of coconut and vanilla in Klappertaart (page 196), a young-coconut tart served with strawberry. Even something as simple as a favourite sambal can trigger memories.

But it's not just about smell or flavour. The experience includes the soft texture of steamed cassava or sweet potatoes, the crispness of fresh vegetables and the creaminess of coconut milk as it coats your spoon. Dishes are colourful and vibrant – palm-leaf parcels filled with turmeric coconut rice, boiled egg and potato sambal; tropical fruits of bright pink, yellow and green; and sauces that bring contrast to every plate.

For me, growing up on the island of Sulawesi, food wasn't just about eating – it was how we connected. It was tradition, celebration and comfort. Clear Spinach and Corn Soup (page 98), sweet and spicy Rujak (page 99) and coconut pudding (page 196) weren't just meals – they were part of the rhythm of life. Sunday mornings often began with *tinutuan*, a golden porridge of pumpkin, corn and water spinach. It was simple but full of care – and to me, it was the taste of home. (You'll find the recipe in my first book, *The Indonesian Table.*)

Our family eventually moved to Jakarta. Towering buildings and busy streets replaced swaying coconut trees and soft, sandy beaches. Above the hum of the city, the air carried a different scent from the endless array of regional cuisines: from Padang and Sunda, West Java to Bali and beyond.

Jakarta was and is a melting pot of Chinese-Indonesian, Arabic-Indonesian, Indian-Indonesian and European-Indonesian influences, all adding to its diverse food culture. It was in Jakarta that I discovered tempeh, tofu, sweet soy sauce and an even wider variety of fermented soy products, different spices and vegetables.

The flavours of Manado – and Indonesian food as a whole – not only connected my past and present but also became a bridge to the future, especially when my family relocated to the UK in 2018. Whether we were amid London's bustling streets or the quiet of our English countryside home, Manado and Indonesia never felt far away. As long as the kitchen was filled with lemongrass, makrut lime leaves, chillies and ginger, I felt at home: grounded, centred and comforted.

That comfort rests on the depth of the culinary traditions themselves. Indonesian cuisine, shaped by centuries of global influences, is filled with many ingredients, some native, others introduced over time. Many of these – nutmeg, cloves, pearl barley, millet, spices, coffee, chocolate, cassava, sweet potatoes, plantains, white and black sesame seeds, chillies – are widely available in the UK. As the country becomes an increasingly diverse melting pot, the demand for such foods will only continue to grow. Since moving back to the UK, I've even noticed how the consumption of the many varieties of tempeh and tofu has mushroomed here, thanks to the global plant-led lifestyle trend.

Some flavours and aromas from your homeland never leave you – they cling to your heart. For instance, the memory of Oma's (grandmother's) food are in a Manado-style *rica-rica* sambal (made with chillies, ginger, shallots, garlic and tomatoes), which I combine with tempeh and pasta (page 83). While it is a modern dish, it still carries the flavour of home. And that balance of heat, sweetness and aroma underpins the recipes ahead.

Such sensory memories live on in every meal, in every bite, in every moment when a familiar dish transports me back to communities in Sumatra, Flores, Bali, Kalimantan, Maluku and the warm shores of Sulawesi – because no matter where life takes you, some flavours and aromas of your comfort food will always whisper: 'you are home'.

A Personal Journey

Over the years, some of my most rewarding experiences as a travelling chef and consultant have been in my exploration of Indonesia's regional cuisines and the incredible variety of ingredients that thrive across its islands. I have spent countless hours in the kitchens of some of the finest resorts and hotels in Indonesia and beyond. Cooking for curious diners has been a chance to share my food and the rich traditions of Indonesian gastronomy.

That passion reached new heights during the G20 Conference. I had the honour of cooking for the spouses of world leaders in Bali in 2022. The plant-led menu featured nearly 50 ingredients in a single lunch. Guests were welcomed with oven-baked tempeh-sago chips and melinjo nut and millet crackers, served with lontar palm fruit salsa, dips made with pili and cashew nuts and nipa palm tree salt from Papua. They were accompanied by June-plum juice infused with lontar blossom cordial.

The menu told its own story through technique and discovery. The appetiser was a tropical salad with mango, rose guava, jicama, snake fruit, pomelo and wild oxalis leaves, known as *rujak* (my version is on page 174). The main course consisted of four small tasting dishes and the dessert was a mini Balinese pancake with pandan and freshly grated coconut, sweetened with palm sugar syrup *(laklak).* I fell in love with a traditional cooking technique of using a clay pot with holes and a beautiful lid for each individual compartment. The experience was deeply educational because I was working with rare ingredients like *cempedak* (a cousin of jackfruit), banana blossoms, coconut blossom and wild greens like moringa and kencur leaves *(daun kencur).*

Links to the past deepened the experience even further. Some of the ingredients used at this lunch are also depicted in the ancient reliefs of Borobudur, the eighth-century temple in Central Java. Written records of early Indonesian gastronomy are scarce and Borobudur's carvings offer a glimpse into the plant-based diets of the past. With a knowledgeable guide, one can uncover centuries of culinary history hidden in the temple's reliefs.

There is always a team behind every memorable meal. It was an honour to collaborate with the trail-blazing entrepreneur Helianti Hilman and her team at Javara, a social enterprise that works with 50,000 farmers across Indonesia to champion forgotten plant-based ingredients. It was also a privilege to work alongside chef Wayan Kreshna Yasa and his team for this unforgettable service. Of course, there were many people involved with the Bali G20 event, and I thank each of them.

Over the past three years, I've come to realise that my travels across the vast archipelago were more than an adventure – they were an education in plant-based diversity. With over 280 million people, 1,000 ethnic groups and 700 languages across three time zones, Indonesia offers an unparalleled wealth of culinary traditions and an abundance of ingredients at our fingertips. This makes it all the more surprising that we continue to import soybeans, rice and wheat flour (a key ingredient for making instant noodles), even though our homeland is so agriculturally rich. It's a gentle reminder of the potential we have to look inward, to grow more consciously and to celebrate the bounty that has always been ours.

My connection to Indonesia has only deepened over time. Every assignment back home is an opportunity to immerse myself in local traditions and discover new ingredients that inspire my work. From Tempeh Laksa (page 89) to Serombotan (Vegetables with a Spiced Coconut and Peanut Sauce, page 108), Indonesia has long mastered the art of plant-based cuisine. At home, I often reimagine these classics in a modern context.

In Indonesia, plant-forward diets have always been a way of life. It lives in the daily ritual of fresh coconut milk, tempeh, turmeric-stained fingers and chillies crushed using a stone mortar for making paste and sambal. It is found in the richness of *gado-gado*, the creaminess of Jackfruit Rendang (page 180) and the sweetness of palm sugar in countless *kolak* variations. Visiting my grandparents' coconut plantation in Manado and standing beneath the same coconut trees that shaded my childhood, I feel a quiet optimism: Indonesia is not just home but a vibrant centre for the plant-based movement – and a healthy, well-nourished future.

The Archipelago of Plenty

Indonesia's native spices and fertile land have attracted global attention for centuries. It is, after all, the birthplace of nutmeg and cloves and a key source for cinnamon and black and white peppercorns – spices that had European traders and, earlier, Chinese and Indian merchants flocking to its shores. That history of exchange was built on more than spice alone.

The country's volcanic soils nurture an incredible variety of fruits, vegetables and herbs as well as three major commodities: coffee, chocolate and tea. Indonesia's mangoes range from golden-fleshed varieties with hints of pineapple and coconut to tangy white ones reminiscent of soursop. Papaya, rich in fibre and antioxidants, is a staple, while coconut provides both carbohydrates and protein. Vegetables, such as moringa leaves, papaya leaves and banana blossoms, along with fragrant herbs like lemongrass, turmeric and galangal, are central to Indonesian cooking.

Among these gifts, one ingredient stands apart. Indonesia's warm climate led to the natural discovery of tempeh, a nutrient-rich, fibre-packed superfood first recorded in Java in the seventeenth century. The birth of tempeh on the island is a remarkable contribution to the growing global movement toward plant-based eating. This humble fermented soybean cake (made using the natural Rhizopus mould) is nothing short of revolutionary.

Javanese communities had been crafting tempeh for centuries, recognizing its ability to provide a sustainable, protein-packed food source. Its firm texture, earthy flavour and versatility have made it a staple not only in traditional Indonesian cuisine but also in modern plant-based cooking worldwide. Java, often referred to as an island of abundance, has given the world a culinary gem that continues to shape and inspire sustainable eating today. Once a humble home staple, tempeh is now prized worldwide by vegetarians and vegans.

Flavour, however, is never carried by one ingredient alone. No discussion of Indonesian plant-based food is complete without sambal. These fiery condiments – made with chillies, tomatoes, shallots and other plant-based ingredients – are essential to our cuisine, enhancing and deepening flavour to savoury dishes. I use sambal not only as a condiment but also as a staple to create modern Indonesian dishes.

Beyond nourishment, plants have long shaped traditional cooking methods and presentation. Hollowed-out bamboo serves as a natural vessel for steaming rice, and banana leaves are used to wrap a variety of ingredients – from tempeh to sticky rice – for grilling or steaming. These plant-based tools are not only biodegradable and renewable, but they also infuse subtle flavours while reducing the need for disposable packaging. Edible leaves, flowers, tubers and grains – including over 200 varieties of rice – bring colour, texture and nutritional depth to dishes. Fragrant red and brown rice lend a nutty aroma, while black glutinous rice often stars in a sweet treat (page 197).

Looking back, I see how each flavour and memory has shaped the way I cook today. From the warmth of family kitchens in Sulawesi to the discoveries of my travels, food has always been my way of making sense of place and connection. This book is a continuation of that path – a collection of recipes that honour tradition while opening space for adaptation and creativity. My hope is that, as you cook through these pages, you will not only taste the richness of Indonesia but also find your own sense of belonging at the table.

Indonesia's Spice Trade

Visiting the Banda Islands was like stepping back in time to the heart of the sixteenth-century spice trade. As I wandered through the streets, I sensed the echoes of history: European traders vying for control over the world's only source of nutmeg and mace. The scent of nutmeg trees filled the air as I explored lush plantations with giant pili nut trees, their gnarled roots a testament to centuries of cultivation. Fort Belgica, standing proudly atop a hill, with breath-taking views of the Banda Sea, reminded me of fierce fighting, lost lives and the dark history of battles fought over these precious spices. My husband and I visited the famous Run Island. We stopped at a small *warung* (a small eatery), and from afar, I saw a young girl lowering a bucket on a line to draw water from a well. There has been little development in the region over the past 500 years, especially considering that the island played such a pivotal role in world history, trade and global cuisine through its prized nutmeg. I couldn't help but wonder if the girl knew the history of her precious island.

Indonesia's spice trade established its culinary identity long before European explorers arrived. Since the first century BCE, traders from India, China and the Middle East introduced ingredients such as rice, garlic, turmeric, ginger and soybeans to Indonesia. Later, the Portuguese and Spanish explorers introduced chillies from South America, now central to Indonesian cooking, especially in the beloved condiment of sambal.

Indian traders brought Hindu and Buddhist influences, which flourished in Bali and encouraged plant-based eating through religious practices. Many Balinese ceremonial offerings to the gods feature rice, vegetables and tropical fruits. In Sumatra, Indian and Middle Eastern spices, combined with coconut milk, gave rise to rich dishes like Roasted Vegetable, Smoked Tofu and Coconut Curry (page 173). Meanwhile, in Sulawesi – my birthplace – the blend of chillies and fragrant coconut defines the bold, aromatic flavours of many local recipes.

The Srivijaya Kingdom (seventh–thirteenth centuries) and Majapahit Kingdom (thirteenth–sixteenth centuries) connected the Nusantara archipelago – modern-day Indonesia – with China, Vietnam, Cambodia, Malaysia and Thailand, spreading cultural and culinary influences. Later, the rise of Islamic states along Java's northern coast introduced new spices and cooking techniques, enriching Indonesia's diverse plant-based food traditions.

The Garden of the World

Cuisine is fluid and ever-evolving. Throughout history, recipes adapt to new ingredients, techniques and cultural influences. Dishes we often associate with a particular culture may, in fact, have deep-rooted connections to other regions or countries, reflecting centuries of migration, colonisation and trade. The movement of people and goods along historic trade routes introduced unfamiliar spices, grains and cooking methods to distant lands, forever altering local culinary traditions. These exchanges did not just shape the course of history – they defined the very essence of our food, demonstrating that cuisine is not static but a living, breathing testament to human connection and creativity.

My fascination with this topic is deeply rooted in plant-based ingredients, especially those that have shaped global cuisine. It began with the realization that nutmeg and cloves – both native to Indonesia – have played a vital role in culinary and trade history, spreading their influence across continents. Even with ingredients brought into the country, like soybeans, we've made them our own. Tempeh, for example – developed on the island of Java – is a uniquely Indonesian innovation, transforming a foreign crop into a beloved and original staple of our culinary identity.

Two Grandmothers, One Table

I have two grandmothers: Oma Merey, my maternal grandmother, who has Chinese, Bugis and Malay ancestry, and Oma Teckla, my paternal grandmother, who has Dutch ancestry. Like many Indonesians, I grew up surrounded by a variety of foods with diverse flavours from a young age. Most Indonesians have ancestors from different parts of the world, and this diversity is reflected in regional Indonesian cuisine. Indonesia's ingredients and techniques also connect deeply to global culinary traditions.

Some ingredients are uniquely Indonesian, such as sweet soy sauce, fermented cassava and rice, tempeh, distinctive spice pastes and the hundreds of vibrant sambals. Certain spices and herbs, such as *andaliman* (a relative of Szechuan pepper), long pepper and ginger flower, also add authenticity to many dishes. I encourage you to keep fresh chillies, crushed chilli flakes or chilli powder on hand, as they are essential for making sambal and are truly integral to Indonesian cuisine.

While the word sambal may not be as globally recognised as hot sauce, salsa or pesto, they all share a similar purpose by adding depth and character to dishes. A great sambal – whether incorporated into a stir-fry, served as a condiment, used as a sauce or even as a salad dressing – is integral to good Indonesian cooking. Shallot Sambal (page 36) is one sambal to always keep on hand – it acts as a simple yet powerful foundation for many Indonesian dishes.

It can be further transformed by adding ginger, tomatoes or pineapple or made into a paste with turmeric, ginger and candlenuts. The balance of sweetness (palm or coconut sugar), salt (salt or soy), sourness (tamarind or lime) and heat (chillies) defines the bold yet harmonious nature of Indonesian cooking. Coconut in its various forms – whether as fresh milk, grated flesh or oil – adds richness, while ingredients like makrut lime leaves and pandan provide distinct floral notes.

Despite its seemingly simple components, Indonesian cuisine carries a depth shaped by centuries of trade and migration. This history makes it easier to find everyday Indonesian ingredients worldwide, allowing home cooks to transform their dishes into a taste of the archipelago. Indonesia's culinary identity, of course, remains deeply rooted in tradition while constantly evolving with global influences. For anyone cooking this food at home, here's the simplest way to stock, substitute and balance flavour.

For the Home Cook

Despite Indonesia's rich culinary heritage, its food remains under-represented globally – even though its abundance of plant-based ingredients aligns with growing interest in vegetarian and vegan diets. The variety is remarkable: from everyday coffee, chocolate and tea to more specialist ingredients, such as coconut, tempeh, spices, herbs and natural food colourings. It is no surprise that many foreign chefs choose to establish their businesses in Indonesia, especially in Bali, where high-quality local ingredients are abundant and easily accessible.

This book is organised by ingredient type, with each chapter dedicated to staples that play a meaningful role in Indonesian cuisine: ferments and pickles, tofu, tempeh and even tropical fruits. I also include recipes for coffee as Indonesia is the world's fourth-largest producer.

While I would love to cook exclusively with native Indonesian ingredients, many recipes have been adapted to incorporate more readily available vegetables in supermarkets. This approach preserves Indonesian flavour while keeping the dishes accessible. In turn, some featured ingredients – such as pearl barley, millet and root vegetables – may feel unusual to Indonesian cooks.

I am delighted to see Indonesian tempeh gaining popularity across the UK and around the world as more producers embrace traditional fermentation methods with local beans. It is now easier than ever to find high-quality tempeh and tofu, making it more accessible to those who want to explore classic and modern plant-based Indonesian cooking.

Let food bring us together.

Glossary

Indonesian vegetarian cuisine is built on a rich tapestry of ingredients – fresh herbs, fragrant spices, tropical fruits and fermented elements that come together to create bold, layered flavours. This glossary introduces many of the essential ingredients used throughout the book, some of which may already be staples in your kitchen. Others might be less familiar but are easy to find at larger supermarkets, Asian speciality food stores or online.

andaliman (lemon pepper)

A wild pepper native to North Sumatra, andaliman is known for its zesty citrus aroma – like a cross between orange peel and mandarin – and a gentle, tongue-tingling numbness. Often likened to Szechuan pepper, but more delicate, it adds an intriguing brightness to Batak dishes. Always used fresh rather than dried, it's a must-try for those who enjoy bold, complex flavours.

calamansi

This sharp yet refreshing citrus fruit can be added to sambals or mixed with water and sugar to make cordial. Calamansi is green when young and ranges from yellow to orange when mature.

candlenuts

This oily nut is often used as a thickening agent and is not recommended to consume raw. I rarely use it and macadamia nuts make a formidable substitute.

cardamom

Indonesian white cardamom has a fresh and distinct aroma that enlivens dishes. It can be substituted with green cardamom, which has a slight peppery note.

chillies

The chilli varieties across Indonesia range in heat level and colour. As they can be difficult to source outside of Indonesia, I substitute them with bird's eye chillies and large red chillies that are mild, fruity and broad in shape. Indonesians also use large, curly chillies to impart colour, rather than heat, to a condiment or dish. In this book, I use the mild red chillies available at most supermarkets.

Chinese celery

Known in Indonesia as *seledri*, this ingredient adds flavour and colour to a dish, but it can be challenging to find. When added to a recipe for flavour, you can substitute it with celery leaves. When Chinese celery is added to a dish solely for colour, I replace it with parsley.

chive roots and stems

Known as *bawang batak*, these are pickled by the Bogor community in West Java. They have a strong garlic flavour when raw but a pleasant aroma when cooked or pickled.

cinnamon

Cinnamon lends a warm, aromatic depth to many traditional dishes, from rich stews like Jackfruit Rendang (page 180) to sweet treats such as Banana and Pineapple Cake (page 200). Its subtle spice enhances both savoury and sweet flavours, making it a cherished ingredient in our culinary heritage.

coconut oil

This was Indonesia's primary cooking oil until the palm oil boom in the 1980s. I mainly use coconut oil for pan-frying or sautéing dishes, but sunflower and rapeseed (canola) oil can also be used. It's worth noting that coconut oil maintains its liquid state above 24°C/76°F. If your coconut oil solidifies, simply melt it gently in a pan.

coconut sugar

Made from pure nectar of coconut blossom, coconut sugar can be used instead of palm sugar.

galangal

A member of the ginger family, galangal is harder than ginger when it is mature. Young galangal has a slightly soft texture with small pink tips. It has a pleasing, soft fragrance and delicate taste compared with ginger.

garlic

Along with shallots, garlic is the basis of Indonesian cooking and is used in most savoury dishes. One variety (*bawang putih tunggal*) has superior health benefits and comes as one large bulb rather than a head with many cloves.

jackfruit

Known as *nangka*, it is enjoyed both in ripe and in unripe form. When unripe, it can be added to curries or *gudeg*, a dried stew from Central Java. In its ripened form, we add the fruit to ice drinks or enjoy it as is. The seeds of ripe jackfruit are delicious when boiled with coconut milk and palm sugar, which is the traditional way to make *kolak*.

kencur

Also known as aromatic ginger or sand ginger, *kencur* is part of the galangal family and used extensively in Bali, West Java and a few Sumatran regions. It has a distinctive fragrance with a pungent and bitter taste, earthy undertones and less spice than ginger and galangal. We tend to use it unpeeled.

lemongrass

We can attribute the fresh and intense tang in our dishes to this ubiquitous ingredient. To release its oil, crush the light green and white parts of larger stems before cooking. The white part can be thinly sliced and eaten raw.

lime

This fruit needs no introduction. Indonesians love using lime for its versatility in cooked dishes and refreshing beverages.

long pepper

Known as *cabe jawa*, this chilli is indigenous to Java and Bali. It has a mild heat, vibrant red colour and soft texture. Nowadays, ripe long peppers are harvested and sun-dried or dried in a dehydrator for a longer shelf life. The Balinese use long pepper most within the archipelago.

makrut lime leaves

A king among Indonesian citrus fruits, the makrut lime has a fine fragrance (though not much juice) and its aromatic leaves lend a citrus note to Indonesian dishes. Available fresh, frozen or dried, they are often added to sambals and satays. Before adding a leaf to a recipe, you must remove the tough centre stem and vein and thinly slice the leaves. In curries and stews, the leaves are torn slightly to release their flavours and then removed before serving. To prepare dried leaves for a recipe, soak them first in hot water for 3–4 minutes.

melinjo (emping) crackers

These thin, delicious plant-based crackers are made from the kernel of the native *gnetum gnemon* plants. Sweet, spicy or naturally flavoured, they make a great accompaniment to *soto*, noodle and rice dishes.

mung beans

These beans are among the most essential pulses (legumes) in Indonesia. We use them in porridge and ice creams and to make glass noodles.

palm sugar

Harvested from a specific palmyra tree, palm sugar is made from the nectar of flowers. (Common Indonesian varieties of the palmyra include *arenga*, toddy palm and *nipa* palm.) The sweet, watery sap drips from cut flower buds.

Once collected, it is heated until thickened and placed in a coconut shell or small mould to set firm. Every island boasts of their own, but good-quality palm sugar should be dark, softly textured and naturally sweet with a hint of toffee. Some are even smoky. You may replace palm sugar with coconut sugar, which has a slightly different aroma and flavour.

pandan leaves

This leaf infuses cakes, drinks and rice with a warm, delicate fragrance and a pale mint green colour. Knot whole leaves first before adding them to recipes. I experimented with replacing pandan leaves using spinach for colour and vanilla extract for aroma – it worked wonderfully.

peanuts

Many Indonesian dishes feature peanuts, from Gado-Gado (page 81) to Peanut Sambal (page 35). They tend to be deep-fried with the skin on, but I opt to roast peanuts (with or without their skin) in a 170°C/338°F/Gas Mark 3 oven for 18–20 minutes, mixing them halfway, for a healthier option. Combine the peanuts with cashews to add a hint of sweetness and creaminess to a sauce.

peppercorns

Peppercorns come widely available in green, black and white varieties. Fresh green peppercorns are fermented and sun-dried to produce hard black peppercorns. While these are used in our cuisine, many Indonesian dishes call for white pepper's distinctive aroma and spice.

pineapple

This delicious tropical fruit features in everything from sambals to curries to desserts, balancing out heavy or spicy dishes with its sweetness and sharpness. When preparing fresh pineapple, Indonesians use a very simple technique. First, cut off the top and bottom so the ends are flat, then trim off the skin around the sides. Look carefully and you'll notice that the inedible eyes spiral around the pineapple. Using a paring knife, remove the eyes by cutting away at them, making V-shaped trenches as you rotate the pineapple. This creates a decorative whole pineapple.

sago flour

This indigenous Indonesian ingredient has been a part of the cuisine for centuries. It is made from the refined extract of a sago palm tree, while cassava or tapioca flour is made of an extract of cassava root. Both flours function as a gluten-free thickening agent, though you could replace either with cornflour (cornstarch) at a pinch.

salam leaves

These aromatic leaves have a subtle woody flavour, generally functioning similarly to bay leaves. Use bay leaves if salam leaves are not available.

shallots

Aromatic shallots are an essential ingredient. With sustainability always in mind, the recipes throughout this book are prepared with the more common banana (echalion) shallots. One banana shallot (approximately 50 g/1¾ oz) is equal to three to four Asian shallots. Shallots are always peeled before use.

Sriracha

A tangy, mildly spicy chilli sauce made from chillies, vinegar, garlic, sugar and salt. Known as *sambal botol* ('bottled sambal') in Indonesia, it is commonly used as a convenient condiment to add heat and flavour to dishes.

tamarind

The fruit grows everywhere in Indonesia. Unripe green tamarind adds sourness to the Jakartan and West Javanese vegetable dish known as *sayur asem*. Ripe tamarind has a sticky pulp used to make Tamarind Paste or Tamarind Water (both on page 32).

tapai yeast (ragi tape)

This traditional Indonesian fermentation starter is used to make *tapai* – a sweet, fermented dish made from glutinous rice, cassava (page 45) or other starchy ingredients. Shaped into small, dry discs, it contains a natural mix of yeast and bacteria that helps break down starches into sugars. It can be found in some Asian speciality food stores or online.

tauco (fermented soy paste)

A savoury paste made from fermented soybeans, *tauco* has a rich, salty depth with a pleasantly rustic texture. Similar to miso, but with a funkier, earthier character, it brings umami warmth to stir-fries, braises and sauces, especially in dishes that highlight tofu, tempeh or vegetables.

tempeh

A traditional plant-based protein made from fermented soybeans, valued for its firm texture, nutty flavour, versatility in cooking and high nutritional content.

turmeric

Often adds a unique taste and vibrant colour to dishes. You can replace every 10 g/¼ oz of fresh turmeric with 1–2 teaspoons ground turmeric, depending on quality and strength.

The Essentials

Bahan Dasar

Some of the most rewarding dishes begin not with a finished recipe but with a simple building block – an aromatic paste, a bold sambal or a richly balanced sauce. These are the quiet foundations of Indonesian cooking, the small essentials that make everyday meals deeply satisfying. Having a few of these at the ready means cooking can be more fluid, instinctive and spontaneous.

In this chapter, you'll find the staples I return to most often. A spoonful of White Spice Paste (page 32) can spark the beginning of a comforting rice dish or simmered curry, while a Shallot Sambal (page 36) adds instant heat and complexity to whatever's on the table – whether that's tempeh, vegetables or even a fried egg. These recipes are designed to be made in advance, stored well and used often.

More than anything, these preparations are meant to bring ease and confidence into your kitchen. They are the flavours that shape memory – the smoky edge of Smoked Tofu (page 44), the gentle sweetness of Palm Sugar Syrup (page 37) or the warm perfume of pandan blended into a vivid green Pandan Extract (page 38). Together, they form a toolkit of flavour that allows you to cook with balance and joy.

Pastes

In Indonesian vegetarian cooking, pastes are the soul of flavour – tamarind paste brings a tangy depth to sauces, while white and yellow pastes form the aromatic base of countless vibrant curries and stews.

White Spice Paste
Bumbu Putih

Preparation time: 10 minutes
Cooking time: 5 minutes
Makes about 100 g/3½ oz (½ cup)

- 2 candlenuts or macadamia nuts, coarsely ground (optional)
- 2–3 tablespoons coconut oil or sunflower oil
- 4 cloves garlic, sliced
- 2–3 small banana shallots, sliced
- 20 g/¾ oz fresh root ginger, sliced
- 10 g/¼ oz galangal, thinly sliced

If using the candlenuts, heat a frying pan over medium-low heat. Add the candlenuts and dry-roast for 3–4 minutes. Transfer the candlenuts to a plate.

Combine all the ingredients in a blender and blend into a smooth paste. It is now ready for use in a recipe.

Yellow Spice Paste
Bumbu Kuning

Preparation time: 5 minutes
Makes 115 g/4 oz (generous ½ cup)

- 1 quantity White Spice Paste (page 32)
- 4–6 red bird's eye chillies, coarsely chopped
- 2 large red chillies, coarsely chopped
- 15 g/½ oz fresh turmeric or 1–2 teaspoons ground turmeric

Combine all the ingredients in a small blender and blend into a smooth paste.

Variation:
- **Red Spice Paste (Bumbu Merah)**
  Simply omit the turmeric.

Tamarind Paste
Asam Jawa

Preparation time: 20 minutes
Cooking time: 5 minutes
Makes 100 ml/3½ fl oz (scant ½ cup)

- 50 g/1¾ oz tamarind pulp, torn into small pieces

Put the tamarind pulp into a bowl and add 200 ml/7 fl oz (scant 1 cup) of hot water. Soak for 15 minutes. Using your hand, squeeze the pulp. Strain, then discard the solids.

Put the tamarind paste into a saucepan and bring to the boil. Reduce the heat to medium-low and simmer for 5 minutes. Leave to cool.

Tamarind paste can be stored in the refrigerator for 2 weeks.

Variation:
- **Tamarind Water (Air Asam Jawa)**
  Dilute the tamarind paste in 400 ml/14 fl oz (1⅔ cups) of water.

Sambals

Sambal is more than just a condiment – it's the soul of Indonesian flavour. Made with chilies and a handful of bold ingredients, sambal will add heat, depth and unmistakable character to plant-based dishes.

Almond Sambal
Sambal Kacang Almon

This is inspired by pili sambal.

Preparation time: 15 minutes
Cooking time: 10–15 minutes
Makes 300 g/10½ oz (1¼ cups)

* 100 g/3½ oz (⅔ cup) almonds or pili nuts
* 2 tablespoons olive oil
* 2 cloves garlic, finely chopped
* 1 banana shallot, thinly sliced
* 2–3 red bird's eye chillies, thinly sliced
* 1 large red chilli, thinly sliced
* juice of 1 lime
* salt and pepper, to taste

Preheat the oven to 170°C/338°F/Gas Mark 3.

Place the almonds on a baking sheet and roast on the lowest shelf of the oven for 10–12 minutes.

Meanwhile, heat the oil in a saucepan over medium heat. Add the garlic and shallot and sauté for 2–3 minutes until fragrant. Add the chillies and sauté for another 2–3 minutes. Set aside.

In a blender, combine the almonds, garlic mixture and 200 ml/7 fl oz (scant 1 cup) of water and blend until thick and smooth. If necessary, add a little water. Transfer to a bowl, then add the lime juice. Season with salt and pepper.

Aubergine Sambal
Sambal Terong Sumbal

Preparation time: 15 minutes, plus cooling time
Cooking time: 20 minutes
Makes 300 g/10½ oz (1¼ cups)

* 1 aubergine (eggplant)
* 4 tablespoons coconut oil or sunflower oil
* 4 cloves garlic, finely chopped
* 1 banana shallot, thinly sliced
* 4–6 red bird's eye chillies, finely chopped
* large bunch of basil, coarsely chopped
* ½ teaspoon salt, plus extra to taste

Preheat the grill (broiler) over medium-high heat.

Place the aubergine (eggplant) on a baking sheet. Grill for 20 minutes, turning every 5 minutes, until softened. Leave to cool.

Meanwhile, heat the oil in a frying pan over medium heat. Add the garlic and shallot and sauté for 4–5 minutes. Add the chillies and sauté for another 2–3 minutes. Set aside to cool.

When the aubergine is cool enough to handle, carefully remove the skin and discard. Finely chop the flesh, then add it to the chilli mixture. Add the basil and salt and mix well. Season with more salt.

Boiled Sambal
Sambal Rebus

Preparation time: 5 minutes
Cooking time: 10 minutes
Makes 100 ml/3½ fl oz (scant ½ cup)

- 2–3 red bird's eye chillies
- 1 large red chilli
- 1 clove garlic
- 1 tablespoon sugar
- salt

Bring a small saucepan of water to the boil. Add the chillies, garlic and sugar and boil for 6–8 minutes, until softened. Reserve 4 tablespoons of the water, then drain. Transfer the mixture to a blender and blend until smooth. If needed, add the reserved water to loosen the mixture to the desired consistency. Season with salt.

Variation:
- **Vinegar Sambal (Sambal Cuka)**
  Replace the 4 tablespoons of water with 4 tablespoons of apple cider vinegar or rice vinegar.

Green Sambal
Sambal Lado Ijo

Preparation time: 10 minutes
Cooking time: 10 minutes
Makes 270 g/9¾ oz (generous 1 cup)

- 10 large green chillies, coarsely chopped
- 4–5 green bird's eye chillies
- 2 banana shallots, coarsely chopped
- 1 green tomato, coarsely chopped
- ¼ teaspoon salt, plus extra to taste
- juice of 1 lime
- 5 tablespoons coconut oil

Put all the ingredients except the coconut oil into a blender and pulse until a coarse paste forms.

Heat the oil in a frying pan over medium heat. Add the chilli paste and sauté for 10 minutes until softened and fragrant. Season.

This sambal can be stored in an airtight container in the refrigerator, topped with oil, for 2–3 days.

Tomato and Chilli Sambal
Dabu-Dabu

Bright, punchy and irresistibly fresh, this Indonesian sambal brings together juicy tomatoes, fiery chillies and zesty lime for a raw, no-cook condiment that's ready in minutes. A drizzle of coconut oil rounds out the heat with a subtle richness. It's perfect as a bold dip, a topping for grilled meats or a vibrant side to rice and noodles.

Preparation time: 5 minutes
Makes 200 g/7 oz (¾ cup)

- 3 green or red tomatoes, chopped
- 2–3 red bird's eye chillies, thinly sliced
- 1 banana shallot, finely chopped
- 2 tablespoons warm coconut oil or extra-virgin olive oil
- ¼ teaspoon salt
- Pinch of sugar (optional)
- Juice of 1 lime

Put all the ingredients in a bowl and mix well. Serve.

This sambal can be stored in an airtight container in the refrigerator, topped with oil, for 2–3 days.

Peanut Sambal

Sambal Kacang

Preparation time: 15 minutes
Cooking time: 15–20 minutes
Makes 300 g/10½ oz (1¼ cups)

- 3 tablespoons coconut oil or sunflower oil
- 150 g/5½ oz (1¼ cups) peanuts, with or without skin
- 2 cloves garlic, thinly sliced
- 1 banana shallot, finely chopped
- 3 large red chillies, finely chopped
- 2 red bird's eye chillies, coarsely chopped
- 2 makrut lime leaves, centre stem removed and thinly sliced
- 2–3 tablespoons coconut sugar or palm sugar
- 1 teaspoon salt
- 1 tablespoon Sweet Soy Sauce (page 38)
- juice of 1 lime

Heat 2 tablespoons of the oil in a frying pan over medium heat. Add the peanuts and sauté for 5–7 minutes until the skin begins to peel or the skinless peanuts turn golden. Transfer the peanuts to a bowl.

Heat the remaining tablespoon of oil in the same frying pan. Add the garlic and shallot and sauté for 3–4 minutes. Add the chillies and makrut lime leaves and sauté for 4–5 minutes. Turn off the heat.

In a blender, combine the chilli mixture, coconut sugar and 200 ml/7 fl oz (scant 1 cup) of water. Blend until smooth.

Transfer the mixture into a bowl, then season with salt, sweet soy sauce and lime juice. If needed, add 1–2 tablespoons of water to loosen the sambal. Leave to cool.

Pineapple Sambal

Sambal Nanas

Preparation time: 5 minutes
Makes 300 g/10½ oz (2 cups)

- 2–3 red bird's eye chillies, thinly sliced
- 1 banana shallot, finely chopped
- ½ small ripe pineapple, cut into bite-size pieces
- ¼ teaspoon salt
- pinch of sugar (optional)
- 2 tablespoons melted coconut oil or extra-virgin olive oil
- juice of 2 limes

Combine all the ingredients in a bowl and mix well.

Serve immediately or transfer to an airtight container, top with oil and store in the refrigerator for 2–3 days.

Variation:
- **Cooked Pineapple Sambal (Sambal nanas dimasak)**
  Simply sauté chillies, shallot and 3 cloves garlic (minced) for 4 minutes. Add the pineapple and cook until softened. Add 2 tablespoons granulated sugar and season with salt.

Smoked Tomato Sambal
Sambal Tomat Arap

Preparation time: 15 minutes
Cooking time: 25 minutes
Makes 500 g/1 lb 2 oz (2 cups)

* 3–4 tomatoes, chopped into 1-cm/½-inch cubes (2 cups)
* 2 banana shallots, finely chopped
* 2 large cloves garlic, thinly sliced
* 2 large red chillies, finely chopped
* 4–5 red bird's eye chillies, coarsely chopped
* 4 tablespoons coconut oil or sunflower oil
* ½ teaspoon salt

Combine all the ingredients except the oil and salt in a bowl, then mix in 2 tablespoons of the oil.

Heat a griddle (grill) pan over medium heat. Add tomatoes and cook for 4 minutes. Add the remaining mixture and grill for another 3–4 minutes, stirring regularly to ensure even charring. Set aside to cool.

Transfer the cooled mixture to a blender and blend well.

Heat the remaining 2 tablespoons of oil in a saucepan over medium-low heat. Add the mixture and simmer for another 15 minutes until reduced by half. Season with salt.

This sambal can be stored in an airtight container in the refrigerator, topped with oil, for up to 5 days.

Shallot Sambal
Sambal Bawang

Preparation time: 10 minutes
Cooking time: 10 minutes
Makes 1 small jar

* 2–3 tablespoons coconut oil or sunflower oil
* 3 cloves garlic, finely chopped
* 2 banana shallots, finely chopped
* 3–4 red bird's eye chillies, finely chopped
* 1–2 large red chillies, finely chopped
* ¼ teaspoon salt
* juice of ½–1 lime

Heat the oil in a frying pan over medium heat. Add the garlic, shallots and chillies and sauté for 8–10 minutes until softened.

Season with salt and lime. If storing, be sure to add enough oil to cover the sambal.

Tahini Sambal
Sambal Wijen Putih

Preparation time: 10 minutes
Makes 100 ml/3½ fl oz (scant ½ cup)

* 4 makrut lime leaves, centre stem removed and thinly sliced (optional)
* 2 red bird's eye chillies, thinly sliced
* 2 cloves garlic, finely chopped
* 5 g/⅛ oz kencur or 10 g/4 oz grated fresh root ginger
* 4 tablespoons lime juice
* 3 tablespoons tahini
* salt, to taste

Combine all the ingredients with 6 tablespoons of water. Mix well.

Tomato and Basil Sambal
Tomat dan Kemaangi Sambal

This iconic sambal from Sumba Island can accompany fish, chicken, tempeh, tofu and vegetables. I have reduced the chillies to a more comfortable heat, but feel free to adjust the amount to your preference.

Preparation time: 10 minutes
Cooking time: 25–30 minutes
Makes 500 g/1 lb 2 oz (2 cups)

- 4 tablespoons coconut oil or sunflower oil
- 2 banana shallots, finely chopped
- 2 large cloves garlic, thinly sliced
- 4–5 red bird's eye chillies, coarsely chopped
- 2 large red chillies, finely chopped
- 3–4 tomatoes, chopped into 1-cm/½-inch cubes (about 2 cups)
- bunch of basil, coarsely chopped
- ½ teaspoon salt

Heat the oil in a frying pan over medium heat. Add the shallots and garlic and sauté for 4–5 minutes. Add the chillies and sauté for another 2–3 minutes. Stir in the tomatoes and bring to the boil. Reduce the heat to medium-low and simmer for 15–20 minutes, until reduced by a quarter. Stir in the basil and cook for another 2 minutes. Add salt.

This sambal can be stored in an airtight container in the refrigerator, topped with oil, for 2–3 days.

Variations:
- **Tomato Sambal (Sambal Tomat)**
  Omit the basil.
- **Sweet Soy-Tomato Sambal (Sambal Tomat Kecap)**
  Omit the basil and add 2–3 tablespoons of Sweet Soy Sauce (page 38).

Sauces and Sweeteners

Rich sauces and delicate sweeteners balance Indonesian flavours, lending dishes their signature push-pull of salty, sweet, sour and spicy.

Palm Sugar Syrup
Sirup Gula Aren

Preparation time: 10 minutes
Cooking time: 15 minutes
Makes 250 ml/8 fl oz (1 cup)

- 1 pandan leaf, coarsely chopped
- 300 g/10½ oz palm sugar, coarsely chopped
- pinch of salt

Put all the ingredients in a saucepan, add 100 ml/3½ fl oz (scant ½ cup) of water and bring to the boil. Simmer for 15 minutes until syrupy. Set aside to cool, then strain. The sauce will thicken as it cools. It can be stored in the refrigerator for 1 month.

Variation:
- **Kolak Sauce (Saos Kolak)**
  To make this coconut and palm sugar sauce, combine 150 ml/5 fl oz (⅔ cup) of coconut milk and 100 ml/3½ fl oz (scant ½ cup) of palm sugar syrup. (You can adjust the sweetness to your desired taste.)

Pandan Extract
Sari Daun Pandan

Preparation time: 10 minutes
Makes about 150 ml/5 fl oz (⅔ cup)

- 4 long pandan leaves, thinly sliced
- 150 ml/5 fl oz (⅔ cup) soy milk or water
- 10-12 spinach leaves (for extra vibrancy)

Combine all the ingredients in a blender and blend for 3–4 minutes. Strain the mixture through a fine-mesh sieve (strainer). Use immediately.

Simple Syrup
Sirup Gula

Cooking time: 5 minutes
Makes 500 ml/17 fl oz (generous 2 cups)

- 400 g/14 oz (2 cups) sugar

Put the sugar and 200 ml/7 fl oz (scant 1 cup) of water into a pan and bring to a simmer. Stir until the sugar has dissolved. Set aside to cool, then refrigerate until needed. It can be stored in the refrigerator for 1 month.

Sweet Soy Sauce
Kecap Manis

Preparation time: 5 minutes, plus cooling time
Cooking time: 20 minutes
Makes 150 ml/5 fl oz (⅔ cup)

- 1 star anise
- 1 (2-cm/¾-inch) cinnamon stick
- ½ stalk lemongrass, crushed and tied into a knot
- 100 g/3½ oz palm sugar, thinly sliced, or coconut sugar
- 10 g/¼ oz galangal, cut into 3–4 pieces
- 3½ tablespoons dark or light soy sauce

Combine all the ingredients in a saucepan. Add 3½ tablespoons of water and bring to the boil. Reduce the heat to medium-low and simmer for 15 minutes, until the palm sugar has dissolved and the liquid has reduced by half. Set aside. The sauce will thicken as it cools.

Strain, then pour the sweet soy sauce into a jar or bottle. It can be stored in the refrigerator for 3 months.

Rice and Accompaniments

Rice is the anchor of every Indonesian meal – often paired with crunchy, savoury accompaniments that add texture and boldness.

Rice Crackers
Rempeyek

Preparation time: 10 minutes
Cooking time: 45 minutes
Makes 20

For the paste:
* 2 candlenuts or 3 macadamia nuts
* 1 banana shallot, thinly sliced
* 1 clove garlic, thinly sliced
* 1 teaspoon ground coriander
* 1 teaspoon salt

For the rice crackers:
* 6 makrut lime leaves, centre stem removed and finely chopped
* 1 egg yolk
* 180 g/6 oz (generous 1 cup) rice flour
* 150 ml/5 fl oz (⅔ cup) coconut milk
* 500 ml/17 fl oz (generous 2 cups) sunflower oil, for deep-frying

To make the paste, combine all the ingredients in a small blender and blend into a smooth paste.

To make the rice crackers, combine the makrut lime leaves, egg yolk and rice flour in a medium bowl. Stir in the paste, then slowly whisk in the coconut milk and 100 ml/3½ fl oz (scant ½ cup) of water. Whisk gently until the batter is smooth.

Heat the oil in a wok over medium heat to 180°C/350°F. Using a spoon, pour a tablespoon of the oil along one side of the pan. Carefully tap a tablespoon of the batter, about 4 cm/1½ inches above the oil, onto this oil trail along the side of the wok, so the batter slides into the oil. Deep-fry for 1–2 minutes until golden, then turn it over and fry for another 20 seconds. Using a slotted spoon, transfer the cracker onto a plate lined with paper towels to drain. Repeat with the remaining batter.

The rice crackers can be stored in an airtight container for 2 days.

Steamed White Rice
Nasi Putih Kukus

My grandmother taught me to make rice when I was seven. In many Indonesian homes, we use a simple, time-honoured method: once the rinsed rice is level in the pot, place your index finger so it touches the rice surface, then add water until it reaches your first knuckle. This handed-down trick works regardless of quantity. It's more than a method – it's a quiet tradition, rooted in instinct, love and trust. You can use a rice cooker, but I prefer a simple saucepan.

Preparation time: 5 minutes, plus 15 minutes steaming
Cooking time: 10 minutes
Serves 4–6

- 300 g/10½ oz (1½ cups) jasmine rice
- 1 pandan leaf, tied into a knot (optional)

Rinse the rice under cold running water until the water runs clear. Combine the drained rice, pandan leaf, if using, and 400 ml/14 fl oz (1⅔ cups) of water in a medium saucepan with a well-fitting lid. Bring to the boil over medium heat and cook for 10 minutes, stirring occasionally until the water has evaporated. Cover, then reduce the heat to low and steam for another 15 minutes. Use a fork to fluff up and separate the grains.

Variation:
- **Red or Black Rice**
  Replace the jasmine rice with red or black rice and cook it with 600 ml/20 fl oz (2½ cups) of water, as instructed.

Turmeric Coconut Rice
Nasi Kuning

Preparation time: 10 minutes
Cooking time: 35 minutes
Serves 6

- 20 g/¾ oz fresh turmeric, peeled and grated, or 2 teaspoons ground turmeric
- 300 g/10½ oz (1¼ cups) short-grain or jasmine rice, well rinsed
- 200 ml/7 fl oz (scant 1 cup) coconut milk
- 1 teaspoon salt
- 4–5 makrut lime leaves, torn
- 1 stalk lemongrass, crushed and tied into a knot
- 1 pandan leaf, tied into a knot

Place the fresh turmeric in 7 tablespoons of water. Mix well, then strain into a small bowl. (Alternatively, combine the ground turmeric and water and mix well.) This is your turmeric extract. Set aside.

In a medium saucepan, combine all the ingredients. Pour in 200 ml/7 fl oz (scant 1 cup) of water and bring to the boil over medium heat. Boil for 15 minutes and stir occasionally until the water has evaporated. Cover, reduce the heat to low and set aside for 20 minutes. Remove the lemongrass, pandan and makrut lime leaves. Serve.

Compressed Rice
Lontong

Preparation time: 5 minutes, plus 3 hours chilling
Cooking time: 35 minutes
Serves 4

- 200 g/7 oz (scant 1 cup) short-grain rice, well rinsed
- ½ teaspoon salt
- 3 makrut lime leaves, centre stem removed and thinly sliced (optional)
- 1 teaspoon sunflower oil, for greasing

Put the rice, salt and 600 ml/20 fl oz (2½ cups) of water into a saucepan. Bring to the boil, then reduce the heat to medium. Simmer, uncovered, for 20 minutes, until the water has evaporated. Mix well, then reduce the heat to low and cook for another 15 minutes. Using a wooden spoon, mash the rice until smooth. Stir in the makrut lime leaves, if using.

Grease a small baking dish. Add the mixture and press it into the dish. Set aside to cool, then cover and refrigerate for 3 hours to chill.

Remove from the refrigerator, tip onto a chopping (cutting) board and cut into 2-cm/¾-inch cubes. Serve.

Golden Umami

Golden umami – crispy shallots and garlic chips – lend a fragrant crunch, deep savoury richness and a beautiful golden colour to effortlessly elevate any dish from simple to sublime.

Crispy Shallots
Bawang Goreng

Preparation time: 10 minutes
Cooking time: 10 minutes
Makes 40 g/1½ oz (¾ cup)

- 200 ml/7 fl oz (scant 1 cup) vegetable oil
- 2 banana shallots, thinly sliced
- ¼ teaspoon salt

Heat the oil in a saucepan over medium heat. The oil is ready when a cube of bread dropped in sizzles on contact and turns golden in 10–15 seconds. (Alternatively, use a thermometer and heat to 180°C/350°F.)

Season the shallots with salt. Add half of the shallots to the pan and deep-fry for 3–4 minutes, until golden brown. Using a slotted spoon, transfer the shallots to a plate lined with paper towels to absorb the excess oil. Repeat with the remaining shallots.

Store in an airtight container for up to 2 days.

Garlic Chips
Bawang Putih Goreng

Preparation time: 10 minutes
Cooking time: 5 minutes
Makes 50 g/1¾ oz (¼ cup)

- 200 ml/7 fl oz (scant 1 cup) sunflower oil
- 3 large garlic bulbs (or 100 g/3½ oz), peeled and thinly sliced

Heat the oil in a saucepan over medium heat. The oil is ready when a cube of bread dropped in sizzles on contact and turns golden in 10–15 seconds. (Alternatively, use a thermometer and heat to 180°C/350°F.)

Add the garlic to the pan and deep-fry until golden brown. You have to keep stirring the mixture to have even colour and crunchy texture. Using a slotted spoon, transfer the garlic chips to a plate lined with paper towels and spread out the chips. Set aside to cool.

Store in an airtight container at room temperature for 2–3 weeks.

Fresh and Fermented Staples

Fresh homemade ingredients and traditional ferments are part of Indonesia's living culinary heritage. They bring softness, richness and depth to the table with every meal.

Fresh Soy Milk
Susu Kedelai Segar

Preparation time: 10 minutes, plus overnight soaking time
Cooking time: 15 minutes
Makes 500 ml/17 fl oz (generous 2 cups)

- 250 g/9 oz (generous 1 cup) organic dried soybeans, rinsed well

Soak the soybeans in a large bowl with plenty of water for 10–12 hours.

Drain the beans, then rinse well. Place in a blender, add 750 ml/25 fl oz (3 cups) of fresh water and blend until smooth and silky.

Strain the mixture through a fine-mesh sieve (strainer) lined with muslin (cheesecloth) into a medium saucepan, squeezing well to extract as much liquid as possible. Bring to a gentle boil, then reduce the heat and simmer for 15 minutes. Stir from time to time.

Serve warm or let it cool, then pour into a clean bottle or jar. Store in the refrigerator for up to 3–5 days. Shake well before serving.

Note: In the spirit of minimizing waste, the leftover soybean pulp from this recipe doesn't need to be discarded. It can be repurposed to make Soy Cakes with Feta, Chives and Chillies (page 64) or Stuffed Courgette Flowers with Tomato and basil Sambal (page 62). By-products offer delicious ways to extend the value of your ingredients while honouring a more sustainable approach to cooking.

Variation:
Add ¼ teaspoon salt; 2 tablespoons sugar or honey; 1 pandan leaf; or 1–2 tablespoons vanilla extract for a different flavour.

Fresh Tofu
Tahu Segar

This quick and easy tofu recipe makes the process calm and rewarding. Just add lemon juice, vinegar or nigari – a mineral salt from seawater – to form fresh curds. Each ingredient gives a distinct flavour: nigari creates a delicate texture with a slight bitterness. It is easily found online.

Preparation time: 1 hour, plus overnight soaking time
Cooking time: 10 minutes
Makes 600 g/1 lb 5 oz

- 500 g/1 lb 2 oz (2¼ cups) dried soybeans, soaked overnight in plenty of water
- 4 tablespoons lemon juice or white vinegar or 1 teaspoon nigari

Drain the soybeans, then rinse well. Place half the beans in a high-powered blender, add 1 litre/35 fl oz (4 cups) of fresh water and blend until smooth and silky. Transfer to a large bowl and repeat with the remaining beans.

Strain the mixture through a fine-mesh sieve (strainer) lined with muslin (cheesecloth) to extract the soy milk. Squeeze well to extract as much liquid as possible. It will yield 1.5 litres/50 fl oz (6¼ cups) of soy milk.

Pour the soy milk into a large saucepan and bring to the boil, stirring to prevent burning, then reduce the heat to medium and simmer for 10 minutes. Turn the heat off and slowly stir in the lemon juice. Set aside for 25 minutes until curds start to form and separate from the liquid (whey). If using nigari, dilute it in 4 tablespoons of warm water.

Line a tofu mould with muslin. Pour the curds into the cloth, then fold the edges over and press with a weight to remove the excess liquid. Let it set for 15–30 minutes, depending on how firm you want your tofu.

Once firm, unwrap the tofu and place it in cold water to firm up further. It is now ready to use. Store in water in the refrigerator, changing the water daily to keep it fresh, for 3–4 days.

Smoked Tofu
Tahu Asap

Smoky, fragrant and quietly complex, this Indonesian-inspired tofu uses tea leaves, rice and sugar to create rich flavour without a grill. It's an easy stovetop method that transforms plain tofu into something special – perfect for adding depth to salads, bowls or simple rice dishes.

Preparation time: 35–40 minutes
Cooking and smoking time: 30–35 minutes
Serves 4

- 400–600 g/14 oz–1 lb 5 oz homemade or shop-bought firm tofu, cut into 4–6 slabs
- 4 tablespoons loose tea, such as black tea, oolong or jasmine
- 3 tablespoons uncooked rice
- 2 tablespoons coconut sugar or brown sugar
- 2 (2-cm/¾-inch-long) cinnamon sticks (optional)

Place the tofu in a rectangular container. Place a slightly smaller dish on top and weigh it down with a small mortar or something heavy. Press the tofu for 30 minutes.

In a small bowl, combine the tea leaves, uncooked rice, sugar and cinnamon sticks, if using. Line an old saucepan (the smoking process may stain the base) with a sheet of aluminium foil. Add the tea mixture.

Place a small wire rack or steamer tray above the pan. Arrange the tofu in a single layer on the rack. Cover with a lid, foil or dry kitchen towel.

Increase the heat to medium-high and steam for 7–8 minutes, until you see whiffs of smoke. Reduce the heat to medium-low and smoke for 20–25 minutes. Keep the kitchen well ventilated. Don't open the lid during the smoking process.

Remove the tofu and set aside for 5 minutes. Discard the tea mix.

Tempeh
Tempe

It wasn't until I lived in England that I crafted this iconic Indonesian ingredient. Though I never made tempeh at home in Jakarta, cultivating it yourself is a truly rewarding experience. Using organic half-split, skinless soybeans simplifies the process beautifully.

Preparation time: 20 minutes, plus 2–3 days soaking and fermentation
Cooking time: 1 hour
Serves 4–6

- 500 g/1 lb 2 oz (2¼ cups) dried organic soybeans, split and peeled
- ¾ teaspoon Rhizopus oligosporus yeast or starter (buy online)
- 2 food-grade zip-top bags (or ½ long banana leaf)

Rinse the soybeans in cold water 2–3 times until the water is clear. Drain well and place in a large bowl, then cover with plenty of fresh water. Leave to soak for 12 hours.

Drain and rinse the beans again until the water is clear. Transfer to a medium pan and cover with plenty of fresh water. Cover and bring to the boil, then reduce the heat to medium and simmer for 1 hour. Set aside for 1 hour.

Drain the beans in a sieve (strainer) and rinse once more under cold running water. Spread over a large tray to cool to room temperature and completely dry out.

Sprinkle the yeast all over the beans and use your hands to mix well so they are equally coated. This ensures even fermentation. Fill the zip-top bags with the beans so they will be 2 cm (¾ inch) thick when laid flat. Use a skewer to poke holes in the bags every 2 cm (¾ inches) for airflow.

(Alternatively, cut the banana leaf into 4 pieces, each 20 cm/8 inches square. Divide the beans into 4 portions. Simply fold one end of the banana leaf to create a pocket, then fill it with the beans. Fold the other end to enclose the filling, ensuring both ends are securely sealed. Repeat to make 4 parcels and cover them with a dry dish towel.)

Place the bags in a warm place at 30–32°C (86–90°F). After 24–36 hours, threads of white mycelium fungus should begin to grow and bind the beans together. Don't touch the bags or try to open them. After 48 hours or so, you should have a firm cake of tempeh that smells mushroomy and is easy to slice. It is now ready to use in recipes.

Fermented Cassava
Tape Singkong

Fermented cassava is incredibly delicious with its sweet, slightly tangy flavour and soft, creamy texture. It's amazing to see how simple cassava transforms during fermentation into a fragrant, comforting treat. Enjoy it on its own, chilled, or add it to cakes and desserts for a unique flavour.

Preparation time: 10 minutes, plus 3 days fermentation
Cooking time: 20 minutes
Serves 10

- 1 kg/2 lbs 4 oz cassava, peeled, washed and cut into 15-cm/6-inch lengths
- 5 g/⅛ oz tapai yeast, crushed into a powder
- ½ long banana leaf

Boil the whole cassava in a saucepan of boiling water for 20 minutes, until it is just tender and begins to split. Do not overcook. Set aside to cool to room temperature.

Line a lidded airtight container large enough to fit the cassava with the banana leaf. Evenly sprinkle the yeast over the cassava, one piece at a time, then place it into the prepared container, cover with the banana leaf and close tightly. Cover the container with a clean dish towel.

Place the container in a warm place (32°C/90°F) out of direct sunlight for 3 days to let the cassava ferment. When ready, it should have a soft texture and a sweet, floral fragrance. It can be stored in the refrigerator for up to 3 weeks.

Ferments and Pickles

Fermentasi dan Acar

Indonesia's warm tropical climate is ideal for fermentation, and preserved foods have long been used to deepen flavour in dishes and boost nutrition. From sambals to pickled vegetables to soy-based pastes, ferments are integral to both everyday meals and festive occasions.

Other fermented soy products include *kecap manis*, Indonesia's iconic sweet soy sauce. Made from fermented soybeans, palm sugar (or nowadays cane sugar) and spices, it brings a sweet-savoury depth to dishes such as Nasi Goreng (page 86). Another staple is *tauco*, a chunky fermented soybean paste often used in vegetable stir-fries and braised dishes.

Oncom, a lesser-known fermented food from West Java, is made from soybean or peanut residue (often a by-product of tofu or tempeh production) fermented with mould. It's commonly used in dishes like *tumis oncom* or *combro* – fritters made with grated cassava and spicy *oncom* filling.

This chapter also includes recipes for Tape (page 189), a slightly alcoholic ferment made from glutinous rice or cassava with Saccharomyces yeast. Enjoyed as a snack, in desserts or in cooling drinks like *es campur*, it even makes its way into cakes and baked dishes (page 207).

Fermented sambals and spices are also celebrated here. Even *arak*, the traditional palm liquor found across many islands, reflects Indonesia's rich fermenting heritage. While I don't make arak at home, I've shared recipes such as fermented jamu (page 184) that capture some of its lively, traditional spirit.

One of the best-known examples of fermentation is tempeh, a fermented soybean product that originated in Java but is now found across the archipelago. That said, not all Indonesians grew up with it – my own childhood in Sulawesi, for instance, didn't include tempeh at the table. Because it has become such a key part of modern Indonesian cooking, I've given it its own chapter in this book (pages 75–94) rather than folding it in here.

Pickled Pineapple
Acar Nanas

Delightful and refreshing, this pickle is infused with coconut and spices and makes the perfect condiment for Jackfruit Rendang (page 180). The balance of sweet, tangy and gently spiced flavours makes it just as good alongside grilled tofu, fried rice or even tucked into a sandwich. The pineapple softens as it simmers, soaking up the aromatic broth for a juicy, flavour-packed bite. Coconut milk is often added to this in the province of Aceh.

Preparation time: 20 minutes
Cooking time: 10 minutes

Makes 1 kg/2 lbs 4 oz (about 4 cups)

- 1 tablespoon plus ½ teaspoon salt
- 1 pineapple, peeled, cored and eyes removed
- 2 large red chillies, seeded and coarsely chopped
- 2 star anise
- 2 (4-cm/1½-inch) cinnamon sticks
- 60 g/2¼ oz (generous ¼ cup) sugar
- 4 tablespoons apple cider vinegar

Combine 1 tablespoon of the salt with 300 ml/10 fl oz (1¼ cups) of water in a large bowl. Rinse the pineapple in the brine, then drain and cut into 2.5-cm/1-inch chunks.

Combine the chillies, star anise, cinnamon sticks and sugar in a medium saucepan. Add 3 tablespoons of water and bring to the boil. Boil for 8–10 minutes to infuse, then reduce the heat to medium. Add the pineapple, vinegar and the remaining ½ teaspoon of salt. Set aside to cool. Transfer the mixture to a large jar.

Pickled pineapples can be stored in an airtight container for up to a month in the refrigerator.

Pickled Rambutan

Acar Rambutan

I love fresh rambutan, although its flavour can be a bit one-note. Pickling transforms it – adding spiciness, umami and tang for a more complex twist on this tropical fruit. You can also pickle canned rambutan or lychee, which brings out its fragrant character in just 10 minutes. Incredibly easy to make, enjoy it on its own or toss into salads for a bright hit of sweet-sour flavour.

Preparation time: 15 minutes
Cooking time: 5 minutes

Makes 500 g/1 lb 2 oz (4 cups)

- 50 g/1¾ oz (¼ cup) granulated sugar
- 1 kg/2 lbs 4 oz rambutans, peeled and rinsed quickly
- 2 red bird's eye chillies, thinly sliced
- 1 large green or red chilli, thinly sliced
- 3 tablespoons lime juice
- 2 limes, thinly sliced
- 1 teaspoon salt

Bring 100 ml/3½ fl oz (scant ½ cup) of water to the boil in a saucepan. Add the sugar and simmer until it has dissolved, then leave to cool.

Add the remaining ingredients to the sugar syrup along with 300 ml/10 fl oz (1¼ cups) of water and mix well. Pour the mixture into a large sterilised jar.

Pickled rambutan can be stored in the refrigerator for up to 2 days.

Note: You can replace the rambutan in this recipe with 2 cans of lychees (1.3 kg/3 lb total weight, drained to 450 g/1 lb).

Pages 50–51: 1. Fermented Cassava (page 45); 2. Pickled Pineapple (page 48); 3. Bogor-style Pickles (page 53); 4. Sambal Lu'at (page 136); 5. Tempeh (page 45); 6. Sour Turmeric Drink (page 184); 7. Pickled Rambutan (page 49); 8. Mixed Fruit and Vegetable Pickles (page 52); 9. Sweet Fermented Glutinous Rice (page 189); 10. Pickled Shallots, Cucumber and Chillies (page 53)

①
②
⑨
⑧
⑦

③
④
⑩
⑤
⑥

Mixed Fruit and Vegetable Pickles

Acar Campur

This mixed pickle has a bright, fruity flavour and is highly versatile, pairing beautifully with fried millet, sorghum or noodles. A quick simmer in spiced vinegar adds just enough heat and tang to soften the vegetables while keeping their crunch. Let it ferment at room temperature, or chill it in the refrigerator, for a lively condiment that only improves with time.

Preparation time: 15 minutes
Cooking time: 15–20 minutes

Makes about 1.3 kg/3 lbs (5 cups)

* 40g/1½ oz fresh turmeric, thinly sliced
* 20 g/¾ oz fresh root ginger, thinly sliced
* 10 red chillies
* 4 star anise
* 1 cinnamon stick
* 100 g/3½ oz (½ cup) granulated sugar
* 1 teaspoon salt
* 350 g/12 oz carrots, peeled and cut into bite-size pieces
* 350 g/12 oz cauliflower, cut into very small florets
* 350 g/12 oz pineapple flesh, cut into bite-size pieces
* 100 g/3½ oz shallots, peeled
* 300 ml/10 fl oz (1¼ cups) apple cider vinegar
* 1 tablespoon coriander seeds
* 1 teaspoon cumin seeds
* 2 fresh bay leaves or dried salam leaves

Put the turmeric and ginger into a blender along with 200 ml/7 fl oz (scant 1 cup) water. Blend well.

Transfer the turmeric mixture to a medium saucepan and add the chillies, star anise, cinnamon stick, sugar, salt and another 200 ml/7 fl oz (scant 1 cup) water. Bring to the boil, then simmer for 10 minutes to infuse the spices.

Add the carrots, cauliflower florets, pineapple, shallots and vinegar. Bring back to the boil, then simmer for another 5–7 minutes to soften the pineapple and carrots. Turn the heat off, add the coriander seeds, cumin seeds and bay leaves. Set aside to cool.

Carefully transfer the mixture to a large sterilised jar and leave to cool, then seal. Label and store in the refrigerator for up to 1 month.

Pickled Shallots, Cucumber and Chillies
Acar Bawang Merah, Ketimun dan Cabe Rawit

This sharp and flavourful pickle is often served with fried noodles or Mushroom and Tempeh Fried Rice (page 86). While I typically use banana shallots throughout the book, I've made an exception here, opting for round shallots purely for their visual appeal.

Preparation time: 5 minutes, plus 24 hours pickling

Makes 375 g/13 oz (1½ cups)

- 50 g/1¾ oz red and green bird's eye chillies
- 15 small round shallots or pearl onions, peeled
- 1 cucumber, chopped
- 200 ml/7 fl oz (scant 1 cup) apple cider vinegar
- 1 teaspoon salt

In a large bowl, combine all the ingredients and 400 ml/14 fl oz (1⅔ cups) of water and mix well. Pour the mixture into a large sterilised jar and seal. Refrigerate for at least 24 hours.

Pickled shallots, cucumber and chillies can be refrigerated for up to 1 month.

Bogor-style Pickles
Asinan Bogor

This beloved Indonesian pickled salad is a close cousin of Asinan Jakarta (page 54) and typically served with a spicy peanut sauce. It often includes tropical fruits such as pineapple, mango and papaya, along with vegetables like chive bulbs (I use ones from my garden).

The brine brings a refreshing balance of sweet heat, while lightly spiced sauce takes on a vibrant red hue from mild, large chillies. Traditionally, it's served with large, yellow, curly rice crackers known as noodle crackers. This bright, punchy salad hits all the right notes.

Preparation time: 25 minutes, plus 24 hours pickling time
Cooking time: 15–20 minutes

Serves 8

For the spicy-sour sauce:
- 4 large red chillies
- 2 red bird's eye chillies
- 5 tablespoons sugar
- 3 tablespoons rice vinegar or apple cider vinegar

For the pickling brine:
- 200 ml/7 fl oz (scant 1 cup) rice vinegar or apple cider vinegar
- 100 ml/3½ fl oz (scant ½ cup) Simple Syrup (page 38)
- 1 tablespoon salt

For the salad:
- 150 g/5½ oz Beetroot Tofu (page 59), cut into 1-cm/½-inch cubes
- 2 carrots, grated
- 1 cucumber, seeded and cut into 1-cm/½-inch cubes
- 20 chive stems
- ¼ white cabbage, finely shredded
- 1 pineapple, peeled, cored and cut into 1-cm/½-inch cubes
- 1 jicama or kohlrabi, peeled and cut into matchsticks
- 50 g/1¾ oz (½ cup) bean sprouts
- 50 g/1¾ oz (scant ½ cup) roasted peanuts or cashews, coarsely ground, to garnish (optional)
- chopped chives, to garnish

First, make the sauce. Put the chillies and sugar in a small saucepan, add 200 ml/7 fl oz (scant 1 cup) of water and bring to the boil. Boil for 5–7 minutes until the sugar has dissolved, then transfer the mixture to a blender and blend until smooth. Add the vinegar. Set aside to cool, then refrigerate until ready to serve.

Next, make the pickling brine. Combine all the ingredients in a large bowl. Add 1 litre/34 fl oz (4¼ cups) of water and mix well. Set aside.

To make the salad, bring a medium saucepan of water to the boil, then reduce the heat to medium. Steam the tofu in a steamer basket or bamboo steamer for 10 minutes. Set aside to cool.

Layer all the salad ingredients in a large container, then pour in the pickling brine to cover the ingredients. Cover with a lid and refrigerate for 24 hours.

To serve, place the salad in individual serving bowls or glasses. Drizzle with the sauce, then garnish with the roasted chopped nuts, if using, and chives.

Jakarta-style Pickled Vegetables

Asinan Jakarta

V Ø

The balance of sour, sweet, salty and spicy flavours makes this refreshing street food a favourite, especially on a hot day. Jakarta's rich culinary heritage, shaped by strong Chinese influences, gives the dish its distinctive character. In Betawi cooking it's considered a classic: cabbage, bean sprouts, tofu and cucumber are soaked in a sweet-sour brine and topped with crispy peanuts and crackers. I've added miso to replace the umami of dried prawn (shrimp) powder.

Double the recipe if you like – it keeps well for up to a week, and the flavours deepen beautifully as the vegetables pickle.

Preparation time: 25 minutes, plus at least 24 hours pickling time
Cooking time: 20–25 minutes

Serves 4–6

For the pickling brine:
- 200 ml/7 fl oz (scant 1 cup) rice vinegar or apple cider vinegar
- 100 ml/3½ fl oz (scant ½ cup) Simple Syrup (page 38)
- 1 tablespoon salt

For the salad:
- 250 g/9 oz Turmeric Tofu (page 58), cut into 1-cm/½-inch cubes
- 2 carrots, grated
- 1 cucumber, seeded and cut into 1-cm/½-inch cubes (optional)
- 50 g/1¾ oz (½ cup) bean sprouts
- 1 small red cabbage, finely shredded
- chopped chives, to garnish
- 50 g/1¾ oz (scant ½ cup) roasted peanuts or cashews, coarsely ground, to garnish (optional)

For the spicy peanut sauce:
- 3 tablespoons coconut oil or sunflower oil
- 150 g/5½ oz (1¼ cups) peanuts, with or without skin
- 2 cloves garlic, thinly sliced
- 1 banana shallot, finely chopped
- 3 large red chillies, finely chopped
- 2 red bird's eye chillies, coarsely chopped
- 2 makrut lime leaves, centre stem removed and thinly sliced
- 2–3 tablespoons coconut sugar
- 1 teaspoon salt
- juice of 1 lime
- 1 tablespoon miso paste
- Sweet Soy Sauce (page 38), to taste

First, make the pickling brine. Combine all the ingredients in a large bowl. Add 1 litre/34 fl oz (4¼ cups) of water and mix well. Set aside.

To make the salad, bring a medium saucepan of water to the boil, then reduce the heat to medium. Steam the tofu in a steamer basket or bamboo steamer for 10 minutes. Set aside to cool.

Layer the tofu, carrots, cucumber, if using, and bean sprouts in a large container. Pour in three-quarters of the pickling brine to cover the ingredients, then cover and refrigerate for 24 hours. Put the rest of the pickling brine into a medium container and add the red cabbage. Cover with a lid and refrigerate for at least 24 hours.

To make the peanut sauce, heat 2 tablespoons of the oil in a frying pan over medium heat. Add the peanuts and sauté for 5–7 minutes, until the skin begins to peel or the skinless peanuts turn golden. Transfer to a bowl.

Heat the remaining tablespoon of oil in the same frying pan. Add the garlic and shallot and sauté for 3–4 minutes. Turn off the heat.

In a blender, combine the peanuts, garlic and shallots, chillies, makrut lime leaves, coconut sugar and 200 ml/7 fl oz (scant 1 cup) of water. Blend until smooth. Transfer the mixture to a bowl, then add the salt, lime, miso and sweet soy sauce. If needed, add 1–2 tablespoons of water to loosen. Leave to cool.

Pour the pickled salad into a sieve (strainer) and set aside for 10 minutes to make sure most of the pickling brine has drained off. Place the salad on a large serving platter or individual plates, arranging the tofu on top. Drizzle with the peanut sauce, then garnish with the chives and chopped nuts, if using.

Tofu

Tahu

Tofu (*tahu*) was introduced to Indonesia centuries ago by Chinese immigrants. The word *tahu* itself comes from the Hokkien term *tauhu*. Over time, Indonesians adapted tofu to local tastes, integrating it into both Javanese and broader Nusantara cuisine. Today, tofu is deeply embedded in our food culture, with a wide range of regional varieties offering different textures, flavours and uses.

From white tofu (*tahu putih*), often referred to as Chinese-style tofu (*tahu Cina*) to fried tofu (*tahu pong*), each type has a place in both everyday meals and festive dishes. White tofu is common in soups, stir-fries and deep-fried snacks, and features in dishes like Spiced Tofu Pockets (page 63).

Markets across Indonesia, especially in cities with large Chinese-Indonesian communities like North Jakarta's Pantai Indah Kapuk, are a tofu lover's paradise. One of my favourites is Papaya Supermarket in Blok M, South Jakarta – sometimes called Jakarta's Little Tokyo – where you'll find Japanese-style tofu in delicate, silky varieties ideal for soups or salads.

I'm especially fond of yellow turmeric tofu (*tahu kuning*), marinated in turmeric and sometimes garlic, giving it a golden colour and earthy flavour. It's popular in Java and often used in fried dishes like *tahu goreng kunyit* in Sunda, West Java. One modern way to enjoy it is baked with chickpeas and kale and served with tahini sambal (page 67).

Perhaps my favourite of all is *tahu Sumedang*, a speciality from West Java. It has a crispy exterior and a light, airy interior with small holes that soak up flavour beautifully. Traditionally sold in banana leaf-wrapped bundles inside woven bamboo baskets, it's best enjoyed hot with fresh green chillies. Recently, I have started preparing my own tofu at home (including Smoked Tofu, page 44), which was much easier than I imagined.

Today, tofu is more than a plant-based protein – it's a reflection of Indonesia's rich culinary heritage. Influenced by Chinese origins and shaped by local ingenuity, tofu continues to be a versatile, affordable and nourishing ingredient found in homes across the archipelago. In England, where I now live, tofu is available in many supermarkets, though I turn to Asian speciality food stores or go online for the best selection.

Turmeric Tofu
Tahu Kuning

This is a simple, unfussy way to transform tofu into something bright and fragrant. Simmered with turmeric, garlic, makrut lime and bay until the liquid evaporates, the cubes gain a warm golden hue and mellow savour.

Preparation time: 10 minutes
Cooking time: 40 minutes

Makes 600 g/1 lb 5 oz

- 25 g/1 oz fresh turmeric, coarsely chopped, or 1 tablespoon ground turmeric
- 5 cloves garlic, finely chopped
- 5 makrut lime leaves, centre stem removed
- 5 bay leaves
- 2 teaspoons salt
- 600 g/1 lb 5 oz Fresh Tofu (page 44) or store-bought, cut into 3-cm/1¼-inch cubes

In a blender, combine the turmeric and garlic with 100 ml/3½ fl oz (scant ½ cup) of water.

Bring 700 ml/24 fl oz (generous 2¾ cups) of water to the boil in a wok or saucepan. Reduce the heat to medium-high, then add the turmeric mixture, makrut lime leaves, bay leaves and salt and mix well. Carefully add the large cubes of tofu, one at a time. If possible, submerge the tofu in the mixture. Cook for 40 minutes, turning the tofu after 20 minutes, until the water has evaporated. Set aside to cool.

Serve the tofu as is or use it in another dish.

Beetroot Tofu
Tahu Bit Merah

Beetroot (beet) is ubiquitous in Indonesia. Soaking tofu in fresh beetroot juice is a brilliant way to enhance both its appearance and taste. The deep hue adds striking visual appeal, while its earthy sweetness gives the tofu a unique flavour. The beetroot tofu can be grilled, pan-fried and used in a variety of dishes.

Preparation time:
10 minutes, plus at least
2 hours marinating time

Makes 200 g/7 oz

- 500 g/1 lb 2 oz beetroots (beets), cleaned and halved
- 20 g/¾ oz fresh root ginger
- 200 g/7 oz Fresh Tofu (page 44)

Juice the beetroots (beets) and ginger to yield about 200 ml/7 fl oz (scant 1 cup) juice.

Combine 300 ml/10 fl oz (1¼ cups) of water with the beetroot juice and place in a container. Add the tofu, ensuring it is fully submerged. Leave to soak for at least 2 hours or overnight, until the tofu absorbs both the colour and subtle sweetness of the beetroot. The longer it soaks, the more vibrant the tofu.

Opposite: 1. Turmeric Tofu (above); 2. Fresh Tofu (page 44); 3. Beetroot Tofu (above); 4. Fresh Soy Milk (page 43).

①
②
③
④

Java-style Tofu Omelette
Tahu Telur

A visit to Surabaya in East Java wouldn't be complete without indulging in its vibrant street food scene. *Tahu telur* is a beloved local speciality that perfectly captures the city's bold flavours. Crispy fried tofu is combined with beaten eggs, creating a fluffy yet crunchy texture, and served with a generous drizzle of sweet and savoury peanut sauce. The miso gives it a boost of umami, and it's kept light with toppings of bean sprouts, lettuce and cucumber. It's the perfect dish for a big breakfast or a light lunch.

Preparation time: 10 minutes
Cooking time: 15 minutes

Serves 4

For the peanut sauce:
* 2 cloves garlic, coarsely chopped
* 3 red bird's eye chillies, coarsely chopped
* 100 g/3½ oz (⅔ cup) roasted peanuts or cashews
* 2 tablespoons coconut sugar
* juice of 1 lime or 2 tablespoons tamarind paste
* 2 tablespoons Sweet Soy Sauce (page 38)
* 1 tablespoon miso paste
* ½ teaspoon salt

For the tofu omelette:
* 8 eggs
* 200 g/7 oz Fresh Tofu (page 44), cut into bite-size pieces
* 4 spring onions (scallions), thinly sliced
* 2 large chillies, thinly sliced
* ½ teaspoon salt
* coconut oil or sunflower oil, for frying

To serve:
* 2 heads little gem lettuce, thinly sliced
* 150 g/5½ oz (1½ cups) bean sprouts
* 2 tomatoes, finely chopped
* 4 tablespoons Crispy Shallots (page 41, optional)
* Red chillies, thinly sliced (optional)

To make the peanut sauce, combine all the ingredients in a blender and add 100 ml/3½ fl oz (scant ½ cup) of water. Blend until smooth. Check the seasoning, then set aside.

To make the tofu omelette, crack the eggs into a large bowl and lightly beat. Add the tofu, spring onions (scallions), chillies and salt and mix.

Heat 1–2 tablespoons of oil in a small frying pan over medium heat. Add a quarter of the egg mixture, swirl the pan to coat the base and cook for 5 minutes, until golden brown. Gently turn the mixture over and cook the other side for 3 minutes, until golden. Transfer the omelette to a plate, then repeat with the remaining mixture to make 4 omelettes in total, adding more oil to the pan as needed.

Top each omelette with lettuce, bean sprouts, tomatoes, crispy shallots and chillies, if using. Drizzle with peanut sauce and serve.

Stuffed Courgette Flowers with Tomato and Basil Sambal

Bunga Sukini Isi, Sambal Tomat dan Kemangi

This recipe presents a delicious way to introduce depths of flavour to the leftover soy pulp from making Fresh Tofu (page 44). Whether enjoyed as a standalone dish or incorporated into a larger meal, this dish celebrates creativity in cooking while staying rooted in tradition.

Preparation time: 25 minutes
Cooking time: 20 minutes

Serves 6

- 12 courgette (zucchini) flowers
- 400 ml/14 fl oz (1¾ cups) sunflower oil, for deep-frying

For the filling:

- 8 spring onions (scallions), finely chopped
- 6 eggs, lightly beaten
- 4 cloves garlic, minced
- 1 banana shallot, thinly sliced
- small bunch of chives, finely chopped
- small bunch of basil, finely chopped, plus extra leaves to garnish
- 400–450 g/14 oz–1 lb soybean pulp (from making Fresh Tofu, page 44)
- 200 g/7 oz feta cheese, crumbled
- 5 tablespoons cornflour (cornstarch)
- 1 teaspoon chilli powder
- salt and white pepper, to taste

For the batter:

- 100 g/3½ oz (⅔ cup) plain (all-purpose) flour
- 50 g/1¾ oz (⅓ cup) cornflour (cornstarch)
- 1 teaspoon baking powder
- salt and black pepper, to season

To serve:

- 140 g/5 oz mixed salad
- Tomato and Basil Sambal (page 37)

Combine all the filling ingredients in a bowl and mix well.

Gently open each courgette (zucchini) flower and remove the stamens. Place a tablespoonful of filling inside each one, close the flower and twist the ends of the petals to seal.

Heat the oil in a deep-fat fryer or deep saucepan over medium heat. The oil is ready when a cube of bread dropped in sizzles on contact and turns golden in 10–15 seconds. (Alternatively, use a thermometer and heat to 180°C/350°F.)

In a large bowl, combine the batter ingredients with 100 ml/3½ fl oz (scant ½ cup) water and mix well.

Working in batches to avoid overcrowding, dip the flowers in the batter and deep-fry for 2 minutes. Using a slotted spoon, carefully flip them and deep-fry for another 2 minutes until crisp. Transfer to a plate lined with paper towels and keep warm while you cook the rest.

Serve 2 flowers on each plate with mixed salad. Drizzle with the sambal and garnish with basil.

Spiced Tofu Pockets
Tahu Isi Pedas

This classic Jakarta street food brings back fond memories of my teenage years studying in the city. Golden, crispy tofu pockets are generously stuffed with a savoury medley of vegetables and sometimes rice noodles for a satisfying bite. For an extra kick, serve with whole green chillies or Sriracha. It's nostalgic comfort food at its best.

I use homemade tofu for its colour. If you're short on time, consider purchasing 230 g/8 oz fried tofu puffs, which you can find in most Asian food shops. Simply make a slit along one side of the tofu and stuff the filling into the hollow.

Preparation time: 25 minutes
Cooking time: 10 minutes

Serves 4–6

- 500 ml/17 fl oz (generous 2 cups) sunflower oil, for frying
- 20 g/¾ oz dried rice noodles

For the tofu pockets:
- 600 g/1 lb 5 oz Fresh Tofu (page 44)
- 2 tablespoons sunflower oil
- 200 g/7 oz cabbage, thinly sliced
- 2 carrots, finely grated (200 g/7 oz)
- 4 spring onions (scallions), thinly sliced
- 2 cloves garlic, minced
- salt and white pepper, to season
- Sriracha, to serve

For the batter:
- 100 g/3½ oz (⅔ cup) plain (all-purpose) flour
- 50 g/1¾ oz (5 tablespoons) rice flour
- 2 cloves garlic, minced
- 1 tablespoon baking powder
- ½ teaspoon salt
- ½ teaspoon white pepper

To make the tofu pockets, place the block of tofu on a chopping (cutting) board and cut into 5-cm/2-inch cubes. Slice each cube in half and scoop out the tofu, about 2 cm/¾ inch deep. (Reserve the scooped tofu.)

Heat 2 tablespoons of sunflower oil in a frying pan over medium heat. Add the vegetables and garlic and sauté until slightly softened, then add the reserved tofu pieces and cook for 2–3 minutes. Season with salt and pepper. Set aside to cool.

Put a tablespoon of the vegetable filling into each tofu pocket. Don't worry if it is untidy, as the vegetables will be contained once the tofu pocket is battered and deep-fried. Cover the opening with scooped tofu. Set aside.

To make the batter, combine all the ingredients in a large bowl. Add 100 ml/3½ fl oz (scant ½ cup) of water and mix until smooth and silky. Set aside.

Heat the oil for deep-frying in a wok or deep saucepan over medium-high heat. The oil is ready when a cube of bread dropped in sizzles on contact and turns golden in 10–15 seconds. (Alternatively, use a thermometer and heat to 180°C/350°F.)

Dip a tofu pocket into the batter, then gently lower it into the hot oil. Add 2–3 more to the wok, taking care not to overcrowd the pan. Deep-fry for 1 minute on each side until golden brown. Using a slotted spoon, remove the tofu pockets and place on a plate lined with paper towels. Repeat until all the tofu pockets are cooked.

While the oil is still hot, add the dried rice noodles to the oil. They will cook in seconds and increase in volume. Remove from the oil and place on the lined plate to drain.

To serve, place the fried rice noodles on a serving plate and arrange the tofu pockets on the side. Serve with Sriracha.

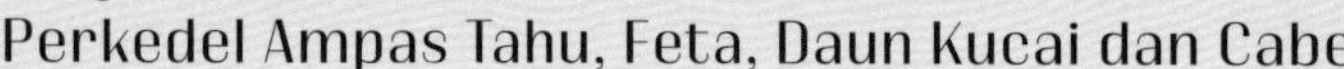

Soy Cakes with Feta, Chives and Chillies

Perkedel Ampas Tahu, Feta, Daun Kucai dan Cabe

Making fermented soy pulp (*oncom*) outside of Indonesia can be tricky due to yeast availability, so using the leftover pulp (*ampas tahu*) from the Fresh Tofu (page 44) recipe is a great alternative. This nutrient-rich by-product can be turned into savoury tofu cakes, which are flavourful, satisfying and waste-reducing. It's a simple way to celebrate plant-based versatility and adapt traditional fermentation practices into something new yet familiar.

Adding yogurt is a nod to the traditional buffalo yogurt I once tasted served in bamboo segments in Bukittinggi, West Sumatra – it pairs beautifully with humble shallot sambal. You can make this dish ahead and reheat it in the oven before serving.

Preparation time: 25 minutes
Cooking time: 20–25 minutes

Makes 14–16 cakes

- 4 spring onions (scallions), finely chopped
- 4 eggs, lightly beaten
- 4 cloves garlic, minced
- 1 banana shallot, thinly sliced
- small bunch of chives, finely chopped
- small bunch of basil, finely chopped
- 300 g/10½ oz soybean pulp (from making Fresh Tofu, page 44)
- 400 g/7 oz feta cheese, crumbled
- 4 tablespoons cornflour (cornstarch)
- 2 tablespoons rice flour
- 2 teaspoons chilli powder
- salt and white pepper, to taste
- 2–3 tablespoons sunflower oil, for frying

To serve:

- 200 g/7 oz Greek yogurt
- 4 tablespoons Shallot Sambal (page 36)
- 1 (100-g/3½-oz) pack mixed salad leaves
- sea salt
- lime juice

To make the soy cakes, combine all the ingredients except the oil and mix well.

Heat the oil in a large frying pan over medium heat. Working in batches to avoid overcrowding, scoop a generous tablespoon of the mixture and carefully lower into the hot pan. Slightly press the mixture with the back of the spoon into a patty shape. Add 3–4 more patties and cook for 2–3 minutes on each side, until golden brown and cooked through. Repeat with the remaining patties, adding more oil to the pan, if needed.

To serve, spread a generous tablespoon of yogurt in the middle of 4–6 serving plates. Using a spoon, create a divot in the centre and add a tablespoon of sambal. Place 3 soy cakes to one side and mixed salad on the other. Sprinkle with sea salt and squeeze a little lime juice over each plate.

Turmeric Tofu, Chickpea and Kale Salad with Tahini Sambal

Tahu Kuning Panggang, Kacang Polong, Kale Dan Sambal Wijen Putih

Feta, chickpeas and kale give a modern twist to Indonesian flavours, layered with Mediterranean influences. The tofu is marinated in turmeric, garlic and makrut lime leaves, then baked until golden – crisp on the outside, tender and flavourful inside. Creamy feta adds contrast, chickpeas bring heartiness and kale adds earthy freshness. Served with tahini sambal, this dish delivers a bold balance of umami, heat and nuttiness.

Turmeric tofu adds great colour and flavour to the dish, but feel free to use store-bought firm tofu if you're pressed for time or want a milder taste.

Preparation time: 30 minutes
Cooking time: 40 minutes

Serves 4

- 5½ tablespoons coconut oil or sunflower oil, plus extra for drizzling
- 400 g/14 oz Turmeric Tofu (page 58), cut into 4 slabs
- 250 g/9 oz kale, stalks removed
- salt and black pepper, to taste
- 1 (570-g/1 lb 4-oz) jar chickpeas with liquid
- 20 vine-ripened cherry tomatoes
- 100 g/3½ oz feta
- 1 quantity Tahini Sambal (page 36)

Make the salad. Preheat the oven to 200°C/400°F/Gas Mark 6.

Drizzle 4 tablespoons of the oil over the tofu. Set aside.

Put the kale in a large bowl and season with salt and pepper. Using your fingers, massage the seasoning into the leaves for 2–3 minutes until softened. Place the kale in a roasting pan.

Partially drain the chickpeas, reserving half of the liquid. Add the chickpeas to the pan of kale. Drizzle with ½ tablespoon of coconut oil, then spread out. Place the tofu, tomatoes and feta in the middle and drizzle with another tablespoon of the oil. Season the tofu with salt and pepper, then bake for 20–25 minutes until the feta and tofu are slightly golden.

Pour half of the sambal over the feta and tofu and gently mix.

Transfer the mixture to a large serving dish. Top with the tofu and feta, then drizzle with more sambal. Serve.

Spiced Tofu in Banana Leaves

Pepes Tahu

I had the pleasure of sampling this dish recently when I visited Bandung in West Java. Cooking with banana leaves is common around the archipelago. In many regions, you'll find different styles of tofu wrapped in banana leaves, often named after the local area where they're made. In this version, I add basil and edamame and serve it with rice.

Preparation time: 20 minutes
Cooking time: 20 minutes

Makes 6–8

* 1 (250-g/9-oz) block Fresh Tofu (page 44), mashed
* 100 g/3½ oz (1 cup) edamame beans
* bunch of spring onions (scallions), finely chopped
* 2 large chillies, thinly sliced
* 1 banana shallot, finely chopped
* 3 cloves garlic, finely chopped
* ½ teaspoon ground white pepper
* small bunch of basil, leaves only
* 6–8 fresh bay leaves (optional)
* salt, to taste
* banana leaves, for wrapping

To serve (optional):

* Steamed Black Rice (page 40)
* Tomato Sambal (page 37)
* Rice Crackers (page 39)
* Stir-fried Tempeh with Chilli, Tomato and Cucumber (page 80)

In a large bowl, combine all the ingredients except the bay leaves, if using, and salt. Season with salt and mix well.

Cut the banana leaves into 15 x 20-cm/6 x 8-inch pieces. Pass the banana leaves briefly over an open flame or steam for 3 minutes, until softened. Spoon 2 tablespoons of the tofu mixture into each piece of banana leaf, then fold and secure both ends with toothpicks to form small parcels.

Arrange the wrapped parcels in a steamer. Steam for 20 minutes until firm and cooked through, then set aside to rest for 2–3 minutes.

Enjoy hot as is or with steamed rice, sambal and stir-fried tempeh.

Braised Tofu with Mushrooms, Chillies and Sesame Oil
Sapo Tahu

Sapo tahu embodies the rich and bold flavours of Indonesian-Chinese cuisine, and my best friend Juli prepares it for me whenever I visit her in Jakarta. This comforting dish features silky tofu cubes bathed in a spicy, aromatic sauce made with lip-numbing Szechuan peppercorns. Mushrooms are added for richness while spring onions (scallions) give it a fresh contrast. When served with steamed rice and enjoyed with a close friend, the dish transforms a simple meal into a cherished moment.

Preparation time: 10 minutes
Cooking time: 15–20 minutes

Serves 4

- 3 tablespoons vegetable oil
- 4 red bird's eye chillies, thinly sliced
- 4–6 dried large red chillies, coarsely chopped
- 20 g/¾ oz fresh root ginger, minced
- 2 cloves garlic, finely chopped
- 1 teaspoon ground Szechuan peppercorns
- 1 tablespoon cornflour (cornstarch)
- 2 tablespoons sesame oil
- 2 tablespoons soy sauce
- 1 tablespoon Sweet Soy Sauce (page 38)
- 1 tablespoon tauco or miso paste
- 450 g/1 lb medium-firm tofu, cut into chunky pieces
- 100 g/3½ oz oyster mushrooms, cut into chunks
- 100 g/3½ oz shiitake mushrooms, halved
- 1 tablespoon lime juice
- salt and black pepper
- 3 spring onions (scallions), finely chopped, to garnish
- steamed rice, to serve

Heat a wok or medium saucepan over low heat. Add 1½ tablespoons of the oil, then add the fresh and dried chillies. Sauté for 2 minutes until fragrant, ensuring that the chillies don't burn. Remove from the pan and set aside.

Heat the remaining 1½ tablespoons of the oil in the wok over medium heat. Add the ginger and cook for 1 minute, then add the garlic and fry for another minute. Increase the heat to high, add the ground peppercorns and sauté for 5 seconds. Pour in 200 ml/7 fl oz (scant 1 cup) of water and stir. Simmer for 5 minutes.

Meanwhile, combine the cornflour (cornstarch) with 3 tablespoons of water. Add this mixture to the pan, stir and simmer until the sauce starts to thicken. Add the sesame oil, soy and sweet soy sauces and tauco and mix well. Add the tofu, mushrooms and fried chillies. Use a rubber spatula to gently toss the tofu in the sauce and cook for another 8–10 minutes. Add the lime juice and mix gently. Season to taste.

Transfer to a serving bowl and sprinkle with spring onions (scallions). Serve with steamed rice.

Sweet and Spicy Tofu and Broccoli

Tahu Pedas-Manis dan Broccoli

This simple stir-fry balances savoury, sweet and spicy flavours. The tofu – crisp on the outside and tender within – absorbs the rich umami of the sauces, while the broccoli adds fresh crunch and vibrant colour. Chilli heat provides just the right kick, keeping each bite lively. Quick to prepare and full of goodness, this dish makes a wholesome, satisfying meal with minimal effort.

Preparation time: 15 minutes
Cooking time: 10–15 minutes

Serves 4

* 1 head broccoli, cut into small florets
* 2 tablespoons light soy sauce
* 2 tablespoons Sweet Soy Sauce (page 38)
* 2 tablespoons sesame oil
* 100 ml/3½ fl oz (scant ½ cup) sunflower oil
* 1 teaspoon black pepper, plus extra to season
* 1 tablespoon cornflour (cornstarch)
* salt
* 280 g/10 oz Smoked Tofu (page 44), cut into bite-size pieces
* 3 cloves garlic, finely chopped
* 1–2 bird's eye chillies, finely chopped
* 20 g/¾ oz fresh root ginger, finely grated
* juice of ½ lime
* steamed brown rice, to serve
* 2 tablespoons toasted sesame seeds, to serve (optional)

Put the kettle on to boil. Put the broccoli florets in a large heatproof bowl and pour over the just-boiled water to cover. Set aside for at least 7 minutes.

Meanwhile, in a small bowl, combine both soy sauces, sesame oil, the pepper and 4 tablespoons of water. Set aside.

Heat the sunflower oil in a large frying pan or wok over high heat. Place the cornflour (cornstarch) in a shallow bowl and season with salt and pepper. Roll the tofu cubes in the cornflour, then add to the pan and fry for 2–3 minutes until golden, turning regularly until crisp. Remove from the pan and set aside.

Remove all but 2 tablespoons of oil from the pan and reduce the heat to medium-high. Add the garlic, chillies and ginger and sauté for 1 minute until fragrant. Stir in the soy mixture and cook for 2–3 minutes until thick and syrupy. Add the tofu, mix well and cook for another minute. Drain the broccoli and add to the pan. Cook for 2 minutes, stirring to coat the broccoli in the sauce. Squeeze the lime juice over the tofu and broccoli.

Serve immediately with steamed rice. Sprinkle over toasted sesame seeds, if using.

Soup Noodles with Samphire, Smoked Tofu and Seaweed Sambal

Mi Kuah dengan Asparaqgus Laut, Tahu Asap dan Sambal Rumput Laut

This isn't a traditional Indonesian dish, yet it feels familiar. The seaweed broth – deeply savoury and slightly sweet – forms the soul of the bowl, enveloping springy noodles in warmth and depth. Seaweed add a briny note that balances the smoky tofu and the natural sweetness of fresh corn. I like to finish with spring onions (scallions).

Preparation time: 15 minutes
Cooking time: 15–20 minutes

Serves 4–6

For the seaweed sambal:
* 5 g/⅛ oz dried wakame
* 1 large red chilli, finely chopped
* 2–3 red bird's eye chillies, finely chopped
* 1 banana shallot, thinly sliced
* 2 tomatoes, finely chopped
* 2 tablespoons lime juice
* salt, to taste

For the soup noodles:
* 2 large leaves pak choy, halved
* 2 tablespoons vegetable oil
* 3 cloves garlic, finely chopped
* 6 spring onions (scallions), coarsely chopped
* 5 g/⅛ oz dried wakame
* 400 g/14 oz Smoked Tofu (page 44), sliced into 1-cm/½-inch pieces
* 100 g/3½ oz fresh corn kernels
* salt and black pepper300 g/10½ oz fresh or cooked dried noodles
* 90 g/3¼ oz samphire

To make the sambal, soak the wakame in 100 ml/3½ fl oz (scant ½ cup) of hot water for 3–4 minutes. Drain, then set aside to cool.

In a medium bowl, mix the cooled wakame with the chillies, shallot and tomatoes.

To make the soup noodles, first soak the pak choy in hot water to soften the stalks.

Heat the oil in a saucepan over medium heat. Add the garlic and sauté for 1 minute until golden. Add three-quarters of the spring onions (scallions) and sauté for 2–3 minutes. Add 900 ml/30 fl oz (3¾ cups) of water and bring to the boil, then add the wakame and smoked tofu and simmer for 10 minutes. Add the corn and cook for 4–5 minutes. Season with salt and pepper.

Add the lime juice to the sambal, then season with salt. Divide the noodles among 4 bowls and top with the broth, samphire and a spoonful of the seaweed sambal. Serve hot.

Tempeh

Tempe

Tempeh is one of Indonesia's most iconic contributions to plant-based cooking. Made from fermented soybeans and a starter culture (Rhizopus oligosporus), it has a firm texture, earthy flavour and a remarkable ability to absorb spices and sauces – much like a braised mushroom. Nutritious and protein-rich, tempeh has long been a staple across Indonesian households and is now gaining global popularity as a delicious, sustainable meat alternative.

The earliest record of tempeh dates to the 1600s in Tembayat Village, Klaten, Central Java. This is supported by Serat Centhini, a 12-volume collection of Javanese tales and teachings published in 1814, which documents everyday life and food culture during the Mataram Sultanate. Today, tempeh continues to evolve – rooted in tradition yet endlessly adaptable.

Tempeh is incredibly versatile. It can be grilled, fried, steamed, baked or crumbled into a range of dishes. In its traditional forms, it can be deep-fried into *tempe goreng*, braised in sweet soy sauce (page 38) or simmered in coconut milk for tempeh laksa. In modern kitchens, it appears baked with garlic, parsley and breadcrumbs, tucked into wraps and burgers or used as a protein-rich base for stir-fries, salads and curries. While soybeans are the most common base, other legumes such as chickpeas (garbanzo beans), black-eyed peas, lentils and butter beans (lima beans) can also be used to create unique variations.

Over a decade ago, I had the opportunity to learn how to make tempeh from Professor Wida Winarno in Bogor, just outside Jakarta. For three generations, her family has dedicated itself to researching, teaching and advocating for tempeh – not just as a humble staple but as a modern superfood with deep cultural roots.

This chapter explores both traditional and contemporary ways to cook with tempeh, celebrating its place in Indonesian food culture and its growing global relevance.

Deep-fried Tempeh
Tempe Goreng

You'll find deep-fried tempeh sizzling in bubbling oil at roadside stalls, markets and warungs across Java. Its rich aroma drifts through the air, luring in hungry passers-by looking for a quick, satisfying snack.

At its core, this simple yet flavour-packed dish of fermented soybean cakes is sliced and fried to golden perfection. The crisp shell gives way to a nutty, tender interior, delivering a delightful contrast in every bite. Paired with fiery sambal, served with rice and vegetables or enjoyed on its own, it captures the heart of Javanese cooking – unpretentious, bold and deeply comforting.

Preparation time: 15 minutes
Cooking time: 5 minutes

Serves 4

* 1 banana shallot, finely grated
* 2 cloves garlic, finely chopped
* 2 teaspoons ground coriander
* salt, to taste
* 1 (200-g/7-oz) block tempeh, thinly sliced
* sunflower oil, for deep-frying
* Smoked Tomato Sambal (page 36), to serve
* Gado-Gado Sauce (page 81), to serve

Combine the shallot, garlic and ground coriander with 3½ tablespoons of water in a large shallow container. Season with salt. Add the tempeh and spread it out to absorb the liquid. Set aside to marinate for 10 minutes.

Heat enough oil for deep-frying in a frying pan. The oil is ready when a cube of bread dropped in sizzles on contact and turns golden in 10–15 seconds. (Alternatively, use a thermometer and heat to 180°C/350°F.) The tempeh will be wet, so carefully lower it into the hot oil and deep-fry for 2 minutes. Turn over and deep-fry for another 1–2 minutes, until golden brown. Transfer to a plate lined with paper towels to drain excess oil.

(Alternatively, you can use an air fryer. Spray each tempeh piece with oil and place in the air fryer, setting the time according to your machine instructions.)

Serve immediately with tomato sambal and gado-gado sauce.

Fried Sambal Tempeh in Lettuce Cups

Sambal Goreng Tempe Disajikan di atas Daun Selada

This dish is sweet, spicy and nutty. In Java and Bali, it's often served with rice alongside various vegetables and proteins as part of *nasi campur* (mixed rice) or added to *nasi tumpeng* – a cone-shaped turmeric and coconut rice dish accompanied by a variety of sides. It also makes a delightful topping for crisp, refreshing baby Cos (romaine) lettuce.

Preparation time: 15 minutes
Cooking time: 15–20 minutes

Serves 4–6

- 400 ml/14 fl oz (1⅔ cups) sunflower oil, for deep-frying
- 1 (250-g/9-oz) block tempeh, cut into sticks
- 4 cloves garlic, finely chopped
- 1 banana shallot, thinly sliced
- 2–3 red bird's eye chillies, thinly sliced, plus extra to garnish
- 10 g/¼ oz galangal, cut into slices 5-mm/¼-inch thick (optional)
- 3 tablespoons tamarind paste
- 3 tablespoons Sweet Soy Sauce (page 38)
- 4 makrut lime leaves, torn
- 2 baby gem lettuces, leaves separated and patted dry, hearts cut into 4-cm/1½-inch strips
- salt, to taste

Heat the oil in a saucepan or wok over medium heat. The oil is ready when a cube of bread dropped in sizzles on contact and turns golden in 10–15 seconds. (Alternatively, use a thermometer and heat to 180°C/350°F.)

Season the tempeh with salt. Carefully lower half of the tempeh into the oil and deep-fry for 6–8 minutes until golden brown. Using a slotted spoon, transfer the tempeh to a plate lined with paper towels to drain. Repeat with the remaining tempeh. Set aside. Cool the pan and oil slightly.

Pour most of the oil into a bowl, reserving 2 tablespoons in the pan. Heat the pan over medium heat. Add the garlic and shallot and sauté for 3–4 minutes until softened. Add the chillies and galangal, if using, and sauté for 3 minutes. Stir in the tamarind paste, sweet soy sauce and makrut lime leaves. Season with salt. Stir in the tempeh and cook for 2–3 minutes. Discard the galangal and makrut lime leaves.

Arrange the lettuce on a serving platter. Fill each leaf with the tempeh mixture, garnish with sliced chillies and serve.

Stir-fried Tempeh with Chilli, Tomato and Cucumber

Oseng Tempe dengan Cabe, Tomat dan Ketimun

This modern version pairs tempeh with yogurt, a classic Central Javanese sambal, crunchy cucumber and fresh tomatoes. For extra texture, add rice crackers on the side. The sambal and crackers can be made a day ahead – store the crackers in an airtight container to keep them crisp. With those prepared, the dish comes together in under 20 minutes.

Preparation time: 10 minutes
Cooking time: 10 minutes

Serves 6–8

* 2 tablespoons coconut oil or sunflower oil
* 2 banana shallots, thinly sliced
* 3 cloves garlic, minced
* 1 (250-g/9-oz) block tempeh, cut into 1-cm/½-inch cubes
* salt
* 2 large green chillies, thinly sliced
* 3 tablespoons Greek yogurt
* 3 tablespoons Tahini Sambal (page 36)
* 1 cucumber, seeded and cut into small cubes
* 10–12 vine-ripened cherry tomatoes
* small bunch of mint, to garnish
* Rice Crackers (page 39), to serve

Heat the oil in a frying pan over medium heat. Add the shallots and garlic and sauté for 2–3 minutes until golden. Add the tempeh and sauté for another 5 minutes until golden brown. Season with salt and mix well. Add the chillies and cook for 1 minute. Set aside.

Mix the yogurt and tahini sambal in a small bowl and season with salt.

Spread the yogurt mixture over a large serving dish. Top with the tempeh and arrange the cucumber and tomatoes on the side.

Garnish with mint. Serve as a starter or as part of a family-style meal with the rice crackers.

Variation:
For a simple take on this stir-fry, omit the tomato, tahini sambal and yogurt.

Winter Gado-Gado with Seasonal Vegetables

Gado-Gado Musim Dingin

I often crave gado-gado in winter – a warm salad drenched in rich, spicy peanut sauce. While gado-gado is traditionally served at room temperature or chilled, this version adds a comforting twist. Warm tofu and tempeh, tender vegetables, potatoes and eggs are paired with a velvety sauce infused with chillies and aromatic spices.

To keep it simple, everything is boiled in one pan, except the eggs, which are cooked separately. The gentle heat of the sauce enhances the flavours and adds cozy warmth – just right for colder days.

Winter gado-gado is a fresh take on a beloved Indonesian dish – nourishing, satisfying and a reminder that even classics can evolve. The sauce can be made a day ahead and gently reheated before serving.

Preparation time: 20 minutes
Cooking time: 25–30 minutes

Serves 4–6

For the seasoning mix:
* 3 cloves garlic, finely chopped
* 2 teaspoons ground coriander
* 1 shallot, finely grated
* 1 teaspoon salt

For the gado-gado:
* 12 new potatoes
* 1 small celeriac (celery root), cut into 2.5-cm/1-inch cubes
* 4 eggs
* 150 g/5½ oz tofu, cut into 1-cm/½-inch cubes
* 100 g/3½ oz tempeh, cut into 1-cm/½-inch cubes
* 50 g/1¾ oz French beans, cut into 1-cm/½-inch segments
* 50 g/1¾ oz (⅔ cup) shredded cabbage
* 1 carrot, grated
* 20 g/¾ oz (¼ cup) bean sprouts
* salt, to taste
* 2 tablespoons Crispy Shallots (page 41)
* 4–8 Rice Crackers (page 39), to serve (optional)

For the sauce:
* 2–3 red bird's eye chillies, finely chopped
* 2 cloves garlic, finely chopped
* 2 tablespoons coconut sugar
* 100 g/3½ oz (scant ½ cup) peanut butter
* 3–4 tablespoons Tamarind Paste (page 32)
* salt, to taste

Make the seasoning mix. Combine the garlic, coriander, shallot and 100 ml/3½ fl oz (scant ½ cup) of water and mix well. Add the tofu, tempeh and salt and mix well. Set aside to marinate for 10 minutes.

To make the gado-gado, boil the new potatoes and celeriac (celery root) in a saucepan of salted water for 12 minutes.

Meanwhile, put the eggs into a small saucepan of cold water. Bring to the boil and boil for 6–7 minutes. Drain, then transfer to a bowl of cold water to stop the cooking process. When cool enough to handle, peel the eggs.

Drain half of the water from the potatoes and celeriac, then return the pan to medium heat. Add the tofu mixture and French beans, cover and cook for 4–6 minutes until warmed through. Add the cabbage, carrot and bean sprouts, then cover again and cook for 2–3 minutes.

Drain the vegetable mixture. Remove the potatoes. Arrange the remaining vegetables on a large serving platter. Cut the potatoes in half and arrange them on the top of the salad. Season with a little salt. Cut the eggs in half, then add them to the salad. Top with crispy shallots.

First, make the sauce. Combine all the ingredients in a saucepan and mix well. Pour in 150 ml/5 fl oz (⅔ cup) of water and mix until smooth. Bring to a gentle simmer for 2–3 minutes. Season with salt.

Serve warm with the peanut sauce on the side and with rice crackers, if using.

Pasta with Tempeh, Chillies, Ginger and Tomato Sauce

Pasta dengan Tempe Cincang, Rica-Rica dan Tomat

I didn't grow up with tempeh, so creating this dish was a real joy. Tempeh rica-rica with tomato sauce pasta makes an unexpected pairing, blending the bold flavours of Manado cuisine with the richness of Italian tradition. The rica-rica sauce is aromatic yet mild, while chewy tempeh brings hearty texture to the pasta. Best of all, it comes together easily in one pan.

Preparation time: 10 minutes
Cooking time: 25 minutes

Serves 4–6

* 400 g/14 oz tempeh, coarsely chopped
* 3 tablespoons olive oil
* 3 banana shallots, finely chopped
* 4 cloves garlic, minced
* 25 g/1 oz fresh root ginger, finely grated
* 2 large red chillies, finely chopped
* 2–3 red bird's eye chillies, finely chopped
* 2 (400-g/14-oz) cans San Marzano tomatoes
* salt and black pepper, to taste
* 400 g/14 oz dried spaghetti
* 12–18 vine-ripened cherry tomatoes
* Handful of basil, leaves only, to serve

Place the tempeh in a food processor and mince for a few seconds.

Heat the oil in a large frying pan over medium-high heat. Add the shallots and garlic and sauté for 3–4 minutes until softened. Add the ginger and chillies and sauté for another 3 minutes.

Stir in the tempeh and cook for another 5 minutes, then add the canned tomatoes and 200 ml/7 fl oz (scant 1 cup) of water. Season with salt and pepper. Add the pasta and spread it out in the pan. Bring to the boil and cook for as long as directed in the pasta package instructions, stirring occasionally.

About 2 minutes before the end of the cooking time, add the cherry tomatoes and cover the pan. When the tomatoes have warmed through, remove them from the pan.

Plate the pasta, then top with the cherry tomatoes and sprinkle with basil leaves. Serve.

Spiced Tempeh and Mushroom Stew
Semur Tempe dan Jamur

The sweetness in this stew – traditionally made with beef – is balanced by a blend of spices, creating a comforting main course usually served with steamed rice. Here, I swap the rice for mashed potatoes to give it a heartier twist.

Like most stews, it requires low heat and slow cooking to develop rich, intense flavours, allowing the tempeh to soak up the spices and broth. It's a dish I love for family dinners and celebrations.

Preparation time: 20 minutes
Cooking time: 1 hour 10 minutes

Serves 4

* 200 g/7 oz sprouting broccoli
* 2 tablespoons sunflower oil
* 3 banana shallots, finely chopped
* 3 cloves garlic, finely chopped
* 2 red bird's eye chillies, thinly sliced
* 20 g/¾ oz fresh root ginger, finely grated
* 2 tablespoons plain (all-purpose) flour
* 2 stalks lemongrass, crushed and tied in a knot
* 4 makrut lime leaves, torn
* 3 green cardamom pods, lightly crushed
* 5 tablespoons Sweet Soy Sauce (page 38)
* 2 tablespoons dark soy sauce
* 2 teaspoons Speculaas spice or five-spice powder
* salt, to taste
* 2 (200-g/7-oz) blocks tempeh, each cut in half
* 4 large Portobello mushrooms, left whole
* 250 g/9 oz vine-ripened cherry tomatoes (still on the vine)
* 4 tablespoons Crispy Shallots (page 41, optional)
* small handful of Chinese celery leaves or parsley, finely chopped

For the mashed potatoes:

* 1.5 kg/3 lb 5 oz floury (baking) potatoes
* 125 ml/4¼ fl oz (generous ½ cup) coconut milk
* 1 teaspoon freshly grated nutmeg
* ½ teaspoon salt

Bring a large saucepan of salted water to the boil. Add the broccoli and cook for 1–2 minutes until bright green and just tender. Drain immediately and transfer to a bowl of iced water to stop the cooking. Drain again and set aside.

Heat the oil in a large, lidded frying pan over medium-high heat. Add the shallots and garlic and sauté for 2 minutes. Add the chillies and ginger and sauté for 2 minutes. Stir in the flour and cook for 3 minutes, then add the lemongrass, makrut lime leaves and cardamom.

Add both soy sauces, then gradually pour in 1 litre/34 fl oz (4¼ cups) of hot water. Mix well, then add the spice blend and season with salt. Mix well, then season with more salt or sweet soy sauce, if necessary. Add the tempeh and bring to the boil, then reduce the heat to medium-low, cover and simmer for 30 minutes.

Add the mushrooms, ensuring they are properly submerged in the liquid. Cover and cook for 20 minutes, then place the cherry tomatoes on the vine on top of the mixture, cover again and cook for another 10 minutes.

Meanwhile, make the mashed potatoes. Bring a large saucepan of water to the boil, add the potatoes and boil for 15 minutes until tender. Drain well, then return to the pan and set over a very low heat for 2 minutes to dry completely.

Heat the coconut milk in a small saucepan until warmed through, then pour over the potatoes. Using a masher, mash the potatoes. (Alternatively, combine the potato and coconut milk in a high-speed blender and blend for a finer texture.) Add the nutmeg and season with salt, then reheat the mash gently.

Plate the tempeh mixture with the mushrooms, broccoli and the cherry tomatoes on the vine. Sprinkle with crispy shallots, if using, and celery leaves. Serve with mash and extra sauce on the side.

Mushroom and Tempeh Fried Rice and Crispy Fried Eggs

Nasi Goreng Jamur, Tempe dan Telur Ceplok

Nasi goreng kebon sirih – a fried rice made with goat meat, seasoned with spices and soy sauce – is one of Jakarta's most popular dishes and the inspiration for this recipe. Here, mushrooms and tempeh take centre stage, transformed by a fragrant blend of herbs and spices.

Preparation time: 15 minutes
Cooking time: 20–25 minutes

Serves 4

* 2 tablespoons baharat
* salt, to taste
* 1 (250-g/9-oz) block tempeh, cut into 1-cm/½-inch cubes
* 3 tablespoons coconut oil or sunflower oil
* 200 g/7 oz assorted mushrooms, such as chestnut (cremini), oyster and shiitake
* 1 quantity Shallot Sambal (page 36)
* 1.2 kg/2 lb 12 oz (7 cups) day-old cooked rice
* 5 tablespoons Sweet Soy Sauce (page 38)
* black pepper, to taste
* 4 eggs
* 2 tablespoons Crispy Shallots (page 41)
* small bunch of mint, leaves chopped
* 6 tablespoons Pickled Shallots, Cucumber and Chillies (page 53)

In a medium bowl, combine 1 tablespoon of the baharat with 7 tablespoons of water and a little salt. Add the tempeh, mix well and set aside to marinate for 5 minutes.

Heat 2 tablespoons of the oil in a wok over medium heat. Add the tempeh and sauté for 3–4 minutes until golden on all sides. Transfer to a plate and set aside.

Heat the remaining tablespoon of oil in the pan over medium heat. Add the mushrooms and cook for 3–4 minutes until softened. Season with salt. Transfer the mushrooms to a plate.

Add the shallot sambal to the pan and cook for a couple of minutes, then stir in the rice, sweet soy sauce and the remaining tablespoon of baharat, using a fork to separate the rice grains and break up any lumps. Cook for 8–10 minutes, until the rice is hot. Season with salt and pepper.

Stir in the tempeh and mushrooms and cook for another 3–4 minutes. Season to taste. Reduce the heat to low.

Meanwhile, fry the eggs.

Divide the fried rice among 4 plates, Top each with a fried egg and sprinkle with crispy shallots and mint leaves. Serve with pickled shallots, cucumber and chillies.

Tempeh Laksa

Tempe Laksa

Laksa is a fragrant, spicy noodle soup that weaves together Chinese and Southeast Asian traditions. In Indonesia, it often begins with rice noodles or vermicelli in a rich broth of coconut milk or tamarind, slowly simmered with spices and herbs. Toppings of egg, crispy shallots, lime and sambal add texture, brightness and heat. Every region offers its own version, yet each carries the same comforting appeal.

Preparation time: 20 minutes, plus 10 minutes marinating time
Cooking time: 35–40 minutes

Serves 4

- 250 g/9 oz tempeh, cut into 1-cm/½-inch-thick slices
- ½ teaspoon salt, plus extra to taste
- 2 tablespoons coconut oil
- 1 teaspoon cumin seeds
- 1 quantity Yellow Spice Paste (page 32)
- 1 tablespoon ground coriander
- 1 teaspoon black pepper
- 1 teaspoon white pepper
- 3 green cardamom pods, slightly crushed
- 4 makrut lime leaves, torn
- 1 stalk lemongrass, crushed and tied into a knot
- 1 tablespoon miso paste
- 600 ml/20 fl oz (2½ cups) coconut milk
- 1–2 tablespoons coconut sugar (optional)
- handful of basil leaves
- salt, to taste
- juice of 1 lime

To serve:
- 2–4 eggs
- 200 g/7 oz dried rice noodles
- 400 g/14 oz (4 cups) bean sprouts
- 2 tablespoons Crispy Shallots (page 41, optional)
- Boiled Sambal (page 34)

Put ½ tablespoon of ground coriander into a medium bowl. Add 100 ml/3½ fl oz (scant ½ cup) of water and ½ teaspoon salt and mix well. Add the tempeh and stir to coat. Leave to marinate for 10 minutes.

Heat a griddle (grill) pan over high heat. Working in batches, add the tempeh and grill for 2–3 minutes on each side. Transfer to a plate. Repeat with the remaining tempeh, then cut into 1-cm/½-inch cubes.

Heat the oil in a large saucepan over medium heat. Add the cumin seeds and cook for 10 seconds, until fragrant. Add the yellow spice paste and sauté for 4–5 minutes. Add the remaining coriander, black pepper, white pepper, cardamom and tempeh, mix well and cook for 1 minute. Add the makrut lime leaves, lemongrass and miso paste. Pour in the coconut milk and 300 ml/10 fl oz (1¼ cups) water. Season with coconut sugar, if using, and salt. Bring to the boil, then reduce the heat to medium-low and simmer for 20 minutes.

Meanwhile, put the eggs into a small saucepan of water. Bring to the boil and boil for 10 minutes. Drain, then transfer to a bowl of cold water to stop the cooking process. When cool enough to handle, peel the eggs and halve them.

Prepare the dried noodles according to the package directions. Drain, then transfer to a bowl of cold water. Drain again, then set aside.

Discard the makrut lime leaves from the broth. Add half of the basil leaves and the lime juice to the broth and cook for 1 minute. Season to taste.

Divide the noodles among 4 bowls. Ladle 2–3 spoonfuls of hot broth into each bowl, then top with the eggs, bean sprouts, crispy shallots and the remaining basil. Serve with boiled sambal.

Tempeh and Tofu Satay

Sate Tempe dan Tahu

I love working with other chefs – collaboration is one of the most rewarding parts of cooking. This recipe comes from Chef Aman, an Indonesian chef of Indian descent who runs a Japanese restaurant in London. We both grew up in Jakarta, and this dish reflects the city's vibrant street food culture.

As night falls in Jakarta, satay vendors fire up their grills, filling the air with smoke and spice. Traditionally made with goat, beef or chicken, satay also works beautifully in vegetarian versions with bold marinades. Aman recommends charcoal for the best flavour, but a griddle (grill) pan or oven grill (broiler) makes a fine substitute.

Preparation time: 15 minutes, plus at least 40 minutes marinating time
Cooking time: 10 minutes

Serves 4–6

* 1 banana shallot, finely ground
* 4 cloves garlic, finely ground
* 1 tablespoon ground coriander
* salt, to taste
* 1 (250-g/9-oz) block tempeh, cut into thick sticks
* 1 (250-g/9-oz) block Fresh Tofu (page 44), cut into sticks
* 120 ml/4 oz (½ cup) vegetable oil
* ½ quantity Yellow Spice Paste (page 32)
* 2 tablespoons coconut milk
* 1 teaspoon coconut sugar or brown sugar
* 1 tablespoon Sweet Soy Sauce (page 38)

To serve:

* squeeze of lime juice
* Herb Salad with Spiced Coconut (page 100)
* Crispy Shallots (page 41), for sprinkling
* Green Sambal (page 34)
* steamed rice

Combine the shallot, garlic and coriander with 100 ml/3½ fl oz (scant ½ cup) of water in a large shallow container. Season with salt. Add the tempeh and tofu and spread it out to absorb the liquid. Set aside to marinate for 10 minutes, turning it after 5 minutes.

Place the marinated tempeh and tofu on a plate and gently dab with paper towels to dry it out. (This prevents the oil from splashing too much during frying.)

Heat the oil in a wok or deep saucepan over medium-high heat. To test if it's ready, drop in a small piece of tofu or tempeh – if it sizzles gently and rises to the surface, the oil is hot enough for frying. Working in batches, carefully lower the tempeh and tofu into the hot oil and deep-fry for 1–2 minutes until golden brown on all sides. Using a slotted spoon, transfer the tofu and tempeh to a plate lined with paper towels to drain.

Remove most of the oil from the pan. Add the spice paste and sauté for 4–5 minutes, until fragrant. Add the coconut milk, sugar and the tempeh-tofu mixture. Mix off the heat for 3 minutes, then set aside to marinate for at least 30 minutes.

Preheat the grill (broiler) to a high heat. Skewer the tofu and tempeh onto thin wooden skewers. Mix a small amount of the leftover marinade with the sweet soy sauce in a small bowl to form a glaze. Grill (broil) the skewers for 5 minutes, turning constantly, until lightly charred, basting with the glaze from time to time.

Serve with lime juice, a sambal of your choice and some hot steamed rice.

Variation:

- **Shiitake Mushroom and Broccoli Satay**
  Keep the mushrooms whole. Cut the broccoli into florets. Soak the broccoli with hot water for 7 minutes to soften. Discard the water and rinse the broccoli under cold running water for 1 minute.

  In a bowl, combine 100 ml/3½ fl oz (scant ½ cup) soy sauce, 3 tablespoons simple syrup (page 38), 3 tablespoons water, 3 tablespoons honey, 2 tablespoons vinegar and 3 finely chopped red bird's eye chillies. Mix well.

  Skewer the mushroom and broccoli onto thin wooden skewers, using two skewers per satay to make handling easier. Dip the skewers into the soy mixture, then grill for 1 minute. Repeat the process – dip and grill – until the mushrooms and broccoli are soft and nicely coated.

  For the final glaze, combine ½ quantity Yellow Spice Paste (page 32), 2 tablespoons sweet soy sauce and the juice of ½ lime. Brush this mixture over the skewers and grill for an additional 20–30 seconds on each side. Serve.

Smashed Tempeh with Green Sambal and Mixed Salad

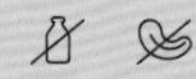

Tempe Geprek dengan Sambal Ijo dan Selada Campur

Geprek means "smashed" in Indonesian. I first tried *ayam geprek* at a restaurant in Jakarta, where a co-founder insisted I order it. The dish, topped with cheese, grilled until melted and served with fiery sambal, had already become a sensation across Indonesia.

The combination of fried chicken, melted cheese and spicy sambal was unexpected yet compelling. It sparked an idea: what if I used tempeh instead? Its firm yet tender texture proved a perfect fit, and by adjusting the sambal's heat I could create a version that's bold but more approachable. This plant-based take honours the original while offering a comforting alternative – and if pounding tempeh isn't your style, it's just as good left whole.

Preparation time: 15 minutes
Cooking time: 20 minutes

Serves 4

* 2 (200-g/7-oz) blocks tempeh, cut each in half
* 1 teaspoon garlic powder
* ½ teaspoon salt, plus extra to season
* ½ teaspoon black pepper, plus extra to season
* 50 g/1¾ oz (⅓ cup) rice flour or plain (all-purpose) flour
* 1 egg, lightly beaten
* 100 g/3½ oz (1 cup) breadcrumbs

To serve:

* mixed salad
* 2 tomatoes, sliced
* Green Sambal (page 34)

Preheat the oven to 190°C/375°F/Gas Mark 5.

Season the tempeh with the garlic powder and ½ teaspoon each of salt and black pepper. Set aside.

Place the flour on a plate and season with salt and black pepper. Place the beaten egg in a shallow bowl and the breadcrumbs on a plate. Dip the tempeh first into the seasoned flour, then into the beaten egg and finally into the breadcrumbs. Place the coated tempeh on a baking sheet lined with baking (parchment) paper. Bake for 16–18 minutes (or in an air fryer for 10 minutes), until golden brown.

One at a time, place each piece of baked tempeh on a chopping (cutting) board, cover with a piece of baking paper and gently crush with a pestle or rolling pin.

Place the crushed tempeh onto serving plates alongside some mixed salad and sliced tomatoes and drizzle with green sambal. Serve.

Stuffed Aubergines with Tamarind

Terong isi dengan asam Jawa

This dish is inspired by *tempeh bacem*, a Javanese-style sweet and savoury tempeh dish that's especially popular in Central Java. Traditionally, tempeh bacem is prepared in large chunks and slow-cooked in a fragrant broth infused with palm sugar, garlic, coriander (cilantro), bay leaves and tangy tamarind. The tamarind adds a distinctive hint of sourness that balances the dish's natural sweetness. While it's typically simmered in coconut water, I've chosen to make this version without.

Here, I've diced the tempeh to help it absorb the spices and tamarind more quickly. The slow braise intensifies the flavours, resulting in a rich, caramelised taste with a subtle smoky sweetness. Instead of serving it with rice, I've paired it with a roasted aubergine (eggplant) boat for a lighter yet satisfying meal. A mixed salad on the side adds freshness and balance to the plate.

Preparation time: 15 minutes
Cooking time: 25–30 minutes

Serves 4

* 2 large aubergines (eggplants)
* 1 tablespoon coconut oil or sunflower oil, for brushing
* salt and black pepper, to taste
* chopped parsley or basil, to garnish

For the filling:

* 2 tablespoons coconut oil or sunflower oil
* 3 cloves garlic, finely chopped
* 2 banana shallots, finely chopped
* 250 g/9 oz tempeh, cut into 1-cm/½-inch cubes
* 100 g/3½ oz chestnut (cremini) mushrooms, sliced into 5-mm/¼-inch pieces
* 2 short stalks lemongrass, crushed and tied into a knot
* 3 makrut lime leaves, torn
* 1 teaspoon chilli powder
* 1 tablespoon ground coriander
* 1 tablespoon coconut sugar
* 4 tablespoons Tamarind Paste (page 32)
* 3 tablespoons Sweet Soy Sauce (page 38)
* salt and black pepper, to taste

For the salad dressing:

* 2 tablespoons light soy sauce
* juice of 1 lime
* 1 large red chilli, thinly sliced
* 1 red bird's eye chilli, thinly sliced
* salt, to taste

For the salad:

* 80 g/2¾ oz salad leaves
* 1 carrot, coarsely shredded
* ½ small cucumber, peeled into ribbons

Preheat the oven to 200°C/400°F/Gas Mark 6.

Cut the aubergines (eggplants) in half lengthwise, then scoop out the flesh from each half, leaving a 5-mm/¼-inch border. Dice the flesh and set aside.

Brush the inside of the aubergine boats with oil. Season with salt and pepper. Place on a baking sheet and cover with aluminium foil. Bake for 20–22 minutes.

Meanwhile, make the filling. Heat the oil in a frying pan over medium heat. Add the garlic and shallots. Cook for 3 minutes. Add the diced aubergine flesh and sauté for 2–3 minutes. Stir in the tempeh, mushrooms, lemongrass, makrut lime leaves, chilli powder, coriander and coconut sugar. Add the tamarind paste, soy sauce and 300 ml/10 fl oz (1¼ cups) of water. Season with salt and pepper. Bring to the boil, then reduce the heat to medium-low and simmer for 20 minutes. Check the seasoning.

To make the salad dressing, combine all the ingredients in a jar, seal and shake well.

Combine all the salad ingredients in a bowl. Add 2 tablespoons of the dressing and toss. Adjust to taste.

To serve, place an aubergine boat on each plate and fill with the tempeh filling. Garnish with parsley. Serve with the salad on the side.

Tender Greens and Salads

Daun Muda dan Selada

This chapter brings together the leafy greens, tender shoots and edible flowers that form the backbone of Indonesian vegetable dishes. While not a botanically precise grouping, it's a practical way to explore the vibrant greens that add colour, texture and freshness to the cuisine, distinct from the heartier vegetables and mushrooms covered elsewhere in the book.

Indonesia's extraordinary biodiversity includes a wide variety of greens that thrive in landscapes from volcanic highlands to coastal wetlands. Indigenous leaves such as moringa, fern shoots, sweet potato, cassava, papaya and amaranth play essential roles in regional cooking, alongside cultivated greens like spinach, water spinach and pumpkin shoots. Edible flowers, including papaya and banana blossom, are also valued for both flavour and nutrition.

These greens reflect a deep connection to land and tradition, and many dishes celebrate their freshness with herbs, fermented ingredients or coconut-based dressings. One unforgettable experience was in Lintau, Sumatra, where women prepared a remarkable rendang with more than 25 different leaves – sometimes as many as 100 for ceremonies – each chosen for its unique flavour and balance.

In this book, I've used leafy vegetables more commonly available in the UK, where I now live, though ingredients like cassava and papaya leaves can still be found in Asian food stores, especially in London. These greens remain central to Indonesian cooking – flavourful, nourishing and deeply tied to place.

Spinach and Corn Soup

Sayur Bening

Simple, healthy and full of heart, this humble yet nourishing vegetable soup is a cherished part of my culinary roots. I vividly remember my grandmother making it whenever she wanted to cook something quick – it was our version of fast food and a staple in many Indonesian households. It's often served with warm rice, tomato sambal and fried tempeh or corn fritters.

Preparation time: 10 minutes
Cooking time: 5 minutes

Serves 4

- 4 g/⅛ oz garlic, thinly sliced
- 20 g/¾ oz fresh root ginger, thinly sliced
- 2 banana shallots, thinly sliced
- 4 fresh corn cobs, kernels removed
- 200 g/7 oz baby spinach
- small bunch of basil, leaves only
- salt, to taste
- 2 tablespoons lime juice
- steamed rice, to serve (optional)

In a large saucepan, combine the garlic, ginger and shallots. Pour in 750 ml/25 fl oz (3 cups) of water and bring to the boil. Add the corn and cook for 3–4 minutes, then add the spinach and basil and cook for another minute. Season with salt and lime juice.

Ladle the soup into bowls and serve as is or with steamed rice.

Mixed Salad with Tamarind Dressing and Rice Crackers

Rujak Campur dan Rempeyek

This refreshing salad offers a vibrant twist on *rujak*, bringing together familiar vegetables in a way that highlights Indonesian flavours. Crisp apple, cool cucumber and peppery radish combine with thinly sliced cabbage. The dressing – a unique blend of tamarind, coconut sugar and chilli – brings the signature boldness that defines rujak.

It's light, punchy and easily adaptable to seasonal produce. The addition of crunchy rice crackers *(rempeyek)* adds extra depth, making it perfect as a starter or a light main. You can also prepare the dressing and crackers ahead of time to make assembly quick and easy.

Preparation time: 20 minutes

Serves 4

For the tamarind dressing:
- 2 red bird's eye chillies, finely chopped
- 100 g/3½ oz (scant ½ cup) coconut sugar
- 4 tablespoons Tamarind Paste (page 32)
- ¼ teaspoon salt

For the salad:
- 1 cucumber, peeled into ribbons
- 2 green apples, cut into long matchsticks
- ½ sweetheart cabbage, thinly sliced
- 6–8 radishes, thinly sliced with a mandoline
- 20 cherry tomatoes
- 10 Rice Crackers (page 39)
- 50 g/1¾ oz (scant ½ cup) roasted cashews, coarsely ground, for sprinkling

First, make the dressing. Combine all the ingredients in a small blender along with 150 ml/5 fl oz (⅔ cup) of water and blend well.

To make the salad, first put the cucumber ribbons into iced water to preserve their crunchiness, then drain.

Arrange the salad ingredients on a serving plate, then drizzle with the dressing. Sprinkle with the ground cashews and serve.

Tip: Add the cucumber core and a few mint leaves to iced water for a refreshing drink.

Herb Salad with Spiced Coconut

Anyang

Anyang is a traditional dish from Sumatra, cherished especially by the Malay and Minangkabau communities. At its core is a mix of finely shredded vegetables and fresh herbs, brought together with a fragrant spiced coconut seasoning.

Some versions also include ground peanuts for extra richness and crunch. What truly defines anyang, though, is the use of fresh herbs. Indonesian wild basil (*daun ruku-ruku*), lemon basil (*kemangi*) and torch ginger buds (*kecombrang*) add brightness, fragrance and a distinctive finish that makes the dish stand out.

Preparation time: 30 minutes
Cooking time: 15 minutes

Serves 4

- 50 g/1¾ oz (scant ¾ cup) desiccated coconut
- 100 ml/3½ fl oz (scant ½ cup) coconut milk
- 2 banana shallots, coarsely chopped
- 4 cloves garlic, coarsely chopped
- 2 large chillies, coarsely chopped
- 2–3 red bird's eye chillies, coarsely chopped
- 2 tablespoons sunflower oil
- salt, to taste
- 4 makrut lime leaves, centre stem removed and thinly sliced
- juice of ½ lemon
- 250 g/9 oz spinach
- 200 g/7 oz sweetheart cabbage, thinly sliced
- 2 carrots, coarsely grated
- 2 pink chicory (endive), thinly sliced
- large bunch of basil, leaves only
- juice of ½ lime
- 3 salam leaves or bay leaves (optional)

To serve:

- Steamed White Rice (page 40)
- Jackfruit Rendang (page 180)

Combine the desiccated coconut and coconut milk in a bowl and leave to soak for 20 minutes.

Meanwhile, in a small blender, combine the shallots, garlic and chillies and blend well. Set aside.

Heat the oil in a frying pan over medium heat. Add the chilli mixture and sauté for 5–7 minutes until caramelised. Add the coconut mixture and salam leaves and sauté for another 5 minutes. Season with salt, then add the makrut lime leaves and lemon juice and mix well. Set aside.

Bring a pan of water to the boil, then add the spinach and cook for 30 seconds. Add the cabbage and cook for another 30 seconds. Drain, then refresh in a large bowl of iced water. Leave for 1–2 minutes, then drain.

Combine the spinach and cabbage with the spiced coconut mixture, carrots, chicory (endive) and basil. Squeeze over the lime juice and mix well.

Serve slightly warm or at room temperature with rice and jackfruit rendang.

Stir-fried Vegetables with Garlic
Cap Cay

Cap cay is a beloved style of stir-fry originating in Chinese Peranakan cuisine but now an Indonesian comfort food classic. The Hokkien term means 'ten vegetables', although it's more about variety than number.

Every region has its own twist, with or without the sauce. I use familiar supermarket vegetables for ease, which gives this version its own identity.

Preparation time: 15 minutes
Cooking time: 15–20 minutes

Serves 4–6

* 1 small head broccoli, broken into florets
* 2 tablespoons vegetable oil
* 1 carrot, thinly sliced lengthwise
* 3 cloves garlic, finely chopped
* 150 g/5½ oz shiitake mushrooms, quartered
* 2 tomatoes, sliced into 3-cm/1¼-inch slices
* 1 spring onion (scallion), thinly sliced (optional)
* 100 g/3 ½ oz sugar snaps
* 175 g/6 oz chard, cut into 1-cm/½-inch pieces (optional)
* 1 teaspoon cornflour (cornstarch) (optional)
* 1 teaspoon lime juice
* salt and white pepper

Blanch the broccoli in a saucepan of boiling water for 5 minutes. Drain and immediately transfer to a bowl of iced water to stop the cooking process. Drain again and set aside.

Heat the oil in a wok or large frying pan over medium-high heat. Sauté the carrot for 1 minute, then add the garlic and cook for another 1–2 minutes. Add the mushrooms and cook for 2–3 minutes, then stir in the broccoli and cook for 3–4 minutes.

Add the tomatoes, spring onion (scallion), sugar snaps and chard (if using) and stir to combine. Add lime juice and season to taste.

Variation:
To add a sauce, combine the cornflour (cornstarch), 100 ml/3½ fl oz (scant ½ cup) of water, salt and pepper. Cover and cook for a final 2 minutes, then stir and serve.

Asparagus with Burrata, Cherry Tomatoes and Olive Sambal

Asparagus, Burrata, Ceri Tomat dan Sambal Buah Zaitun

It wasn't until we moved to Jakarta that I first tasted *rawon sapi* – a rich soup made with *keluwak*, the fermented seed of the pangium fruit. Its deep, earthy flavour and black colour reminded me, later on, of the complexity found in black olives.

This olive sambal captures the same smoky depth of a keluwak sambal. It pairs beautifully with this asparagus and tomato tart. While not traditionally Indonesian, this fusion shows how sambal can bridge cultures, bringing bold Indonesian flavours into new and unexpected settings.

Preparation time: 20 minutes
Cooking time: 30–35 minutes

Serves 6

For the olive sambal:

- 3–4 tablespoons olive oil
- 3 cloves garlic, finely chopped
- 1 banana shallot, finely chopped
- 2 red bird's eye chillies, finely chopped
- 1–2 large red chillies, finely chopped
- juice of ½–1 lime
- 50 g/1¾ oz black olives, halved
- salt, to taste

For the tart:

- 320 g/11¼ oz all-butter puff pastry sheets
- 14 vine-ripened cherry tomatoes, halved
- 16 fine asparagus spears, trimmed
- salt and black pepper, to taste
- 1 egg, lightly beaten
- 250 g/9 oz burrata cheese, roughly torn
- green salad, to serve (optional)

First, make the sambal. Heat 2 tablespoons of the oil in a frying pan over medium heat. Add the garlic, shallot and chillies and sauté for 8–10 minutes until softened. Season with lime juice and set aside to cool.

When cool, transfer the mixture to a small blender. Add the olives and blend well. Stir in the remaining 1–2 tablespoons of olive oil, then season with salt.

To make the tart, preheat the oven to 200°C/400°F/Gas Mark 6 and line a baking sheet with baking (parchment) paper.

Unroll the puff pastry onto the prepared baking sheet. Using a sharp knife, score a 2-cm/¾-inch-wide border around the edge of the pastry, taking care not to cut all the way through. Prick the pastry inside the border all over with a fork to prevent it from puffing up too much in the oven. Spread the olive sambal over the pastry, then arrange the tomatoes and asparagus over the top. Season with salt and pepper. Brush the edges of the pastry with the beaten egg.

Bake in the centre of the oven for 22–24 minutes, until the pastry is crisp and golden. Slice the tart. Top with the burrata and serve with a green salad, if using.

Greens in Coconut Milk, Ginger and Kidney Beans

Sayur Liklik dan Kacang Merah

While visiting a 'living museum' in West Bali – a working village where traditions are preserved and shared – I came across an exhibition exploring the Balinese cycle of life. In one of the main buildings, I found unexpected inspiration: a display dedicated to traditional plant-based recipes. Among them was a simple yet flavourful vegan dish filled with leafy greens, herbs, young coconut jelly and vibrant spices. The mix of tender spinach, fragrant basil, ginger and galangal felt deeply nourishing and beautifully connected to nature. Drawn to its simplicity, I began imagining a modern take, using rich coconut milk in place of young glutinous coconut.

Preparation time: 10 minutes
Cooking time: 15 minutes

Serves 4–6

* 2 large red chillies, finely chopped
* 1 shallot, finely chopped
* 20 g/¾ oz fresh root ginger, grated
* 2 fresh or dried bay leaves
* 1 (400-ml/14-fl oz) can coconut milk
* salt and white pepper, to taste
* 1 (400-g/14-oz) can kidney beans in water, drained and rinsed
* 1 (400-g/14-oz) pack spinach
* 2 tablespoons lime juice
* 2 tablespoons Crispy Shallots (page 41)
* 2 teaspoons Garlic Chips (page 42), crushed
* small handful of basil leaves, chopped

Bring 500 ml/17 fl oz (generous 2 cups) of water to the boil in a medium saucepan. Add the chillies, shallot, ginger and bay leaves and simmer for 8 minutes to infuse.

Add the coconut milk and season with salt and pepper, then add the kidney beans. Bring to the boil, then simmer for 5 minutes. Add the spinach and cook for another 1–2 minutes. Season with salt, pepper and lime juice.

Divide the mixture among 4 bowls and sprinkle with crispy shallots, garlic chips and basil. Serve hot.

Vegetables with a Spiced Coconut and Peanut Sauce

Serombotan

It was a lovely afternoon in February when Chef Switi Nyoman – a colleague and a fearless Balinese chef – drove me from Ubud to the Gianyar food market. The market comes alive around 5 p.m., bustling with stalls selling everything from fish soup to traditional desserts.

One highlight was *serombotan* – heaped platters of blanched vegetables with two sauces. The first is a spiced coconut-turmeric dressing with garlic and fragrant spices; the second, a fiery peanut sauce brightened with chilli and lime. Together they create a bold, balanced flavour – earthy, nutty, spicy and tangy – delicious even without the traditional shrimp paste.

Preparation time: 20 minutes
Cooking time: 20 minutes

Serves 4–6

* 3 salam leaves or bay leaves
* 200 g/7 oz (2⅓ cups) freshly grated coconut (see Note)
* 4 makrut lime leaves, centre stem removed and thinly sliced
* ½ quantity Yellow Spice Paste (page 32)
* salt, to taste
* ½ teaspoon coconut sugar
* 100 g/3½ oz green beans
* 200 g/7 oz sweetheart cabbage, thinly sliced
* 200 g/7 oz spinach
* 2 carrots, coarsely grated
* 50 g/1¾ oz (½ cup) bean sprouts
* large bunch of basil, leaves only
* Peanut Sambal (page 35)

In a saucepan, combine the grated coconut, makrut lime leaves and spice paste and mix well. Cook over medium heat for 10 minutes, stirring occasionally. Season with salt and coconut sugar. Mix well and set aside.

Bring a saucepan with 1.5 litres/50 fl oz (6¼ cups) of water to the boil. Add the beans and blanch for 5 minutes. Meanwhile, prepare a large bowl of iced water. Using tongs, transfer the beans to the bowl of iced water to stop the cooking.

Add the cabbage to the boiling water and blanch for 2 minutes. Add the spinach and blanch for 5 seconds. Transfer the cabbage and spinach to the bowl of iced water.

Drain the vegetables, then slice the beans lengthwise, then cut crosswise into shorter lengths.

In a large bowl, combine the carrots, bean sprouts, basil and blanched vegetables with three-quarters of the coconut mixture. Mix well. Divide among 4 serving plates, then top with the remaining coconut mixture and the peanut sambal and serve.

Note: Freshly grated coconut can be substituted with 50 g/1¾ oz (scant ¾ cup) of unsweetened desiccated coconut soaked in 100 ml/3½ fl oz (scant ½ cup) of coconut milk. Soak for 20 minutes, then set aside.

Spinach and Rice Pasta with Tomato and Basil Sauce

Giling-Giling dengan Bayam, Saus Tomat dan Kemangi

Last year, I took my husband on a road trip to North Bali – a region he had never explored before. Along the way, we visited Rumah Intaran, a centre for architecture and gastronomy run by husband-and-wife team Gede and Ayu Kresna. There, they host a cooking school and a lively Sunday community market. Gede and Ayu welcomed us warmly and treated us to a spread of dishes. One that particularly caught my eye was *giling-giling* – not just for its unique shape but for its vivid green colour. Traditionally a sweet made from rice flour and pandan, it's served with grated coconut and palm sugar syrup.

Inspired by its texture and appearance, I've reimagined it as a savoury pasta dish. With its slightly chewy texture and wholesome ingredients, it's not only fun to make (get the kids involved!) but also incredibly satisfying to eat.

Preparation time: 30 minutes
Cooking time: 20 minutes

Serves 4

For the pasta:
* 50 g/1¾ oz baby spinach
* 200 g/7 oz (1¼ cup) rice flour, plus extra if needed
* 80 g/2¾ oz (⅔ cup) cassava flour
* 2 eggs
* ½ teaspoon salt

For the sauce:
* 2 tablespoons olive oil
* 2 banana shallots, finely chopped
* 4 cloves garlic, minced
* 2–3 red bird's eye chillies, finely chopped or 2 teaspoons chilli flakes
* 1 (400-g/14-oz) can chopped San Marzano tomatoes
* salt, to taste
* 200 g/7 oz baby spinach
* small handful of basil, coarsely chopped
* 100 g/3½ oz mature Gouda, grated, plus extra to serve (optional)

Start with the pasta. In a small blender, blitz the spinach with 50 ml/1¾ fl oz (¼ cup) water. Strain the mixture into a measuring jug.

In a mixing bowl, combine 100 ml/3½ fl oz (scant ½ cup) of the spinach water, both of the flours, the eggs and salt. Mix with your hands until it forms a smooth ball of dough. If it's sticky, add another 1–2 tablespoons of rice flour.

To make the giling-giling, tear off 2-cm/¾-inch balls of dough. Roll them out between your palms into 5-cm/2-inch lengths. Set aside.

Meanwhile, make the sauce. Heat the oil in a frying pan over medium heat, add the shallots and garlic and sauté for 2–3 minutes. Add the chillies and cook for another minute, then add the tomatoes and 300 ml/10 fl oz (1¼ cups) of water. Season with salt, mix well and bring to the boil.

Add the giling-giling, spreading them out and ensuring they are submerged in the sauce. Cover and cook over medium heat for 15 minutes, until the sauce has thickened. Add the spinach, basil and cheese to the sauce and mix well.

Serve the mixture in 4 pasta bowls, sprinkled with extra cheese, if you like.

Water Spinach Noodles
Lomie Kangkung

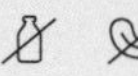

This is one of my favourite noodle dishes, known for its rich broth and vibrant water spinach (water morning glory). It takes me back to my secondary school days, when it was a canteen staple. A Chinese-Indonesian classic, it features thick, chewy wheat noodles in a luscious garlic–soy gravy, sometimes enriched with fermented bean paste.

Traditionally topped with meat, seafood, or quail eggs, here I use shiitake mushrooms, finished with blanched water spinach, crisp bean sprouts and a splash of lime and sambal.

Preparation time: 20 minutes
Cooking time: 30 minutes

Serves 4

- 3 tablespoons sunflower oil
- 2 banana shallots, thinly sliced
- 4 cloves garlic, finely chopped
- 4 spring onions (scallions), coarsely chopped
- 10 shiitake mushrooms, coarsely chopped
- 1 tablespoon white pepper
- salt
- 4 tablespoons Sweet Soy Sauce (page 38)
- 1 tablespoon light soy sauce
- 2 tablespoons cornflour (cornstarch)
- 400 g/14 oz fresh, thick egg noodles

For the toppings:

- 2 tablespoons vegetable oil
- 2 cloves garlic, finely chopped
- 12–15 shiitake mushrooms, sliced
- 2 spring onions (scallions), finely chopped
- salt, to taste
- 125 g/4½ oz water spinach or spinach
- 100 g/3½ oz (1 cup) bean sprouts

To serve:

- 2 tablespoons sesame oil
- 2 tablespoons Crispy Shallots (page 41)
- 2 tablespoons Garlic Chips (page 42)
- 2 limes, quartered (optional)
- Boiled Sambal (page 34) or Sriracha

Heat the oil in a medium saucepan over medium-high heat. Add the shallots and garlic and sauté for 2–3 minutes, until golden and fragrant. Add the spring onions (scallions) and mushrooms and sauté for 4–5 minutes, until caramelised. Pour in 800 ml/27 fl oz (3½ cups) of water, add the pepper and season with salt. Simmer for 20 minutes.

In a small bowl, combine both soy sauces, the cornflour (cornstarch) and 6 tablespoons of water. Set aside.

Meanwhile, prepare the toppings. Heat the oil in a frying pan over medium heat. Add the garlic and sauté for 2–3 minutes, then add the mushrooms and cook for another 2–3 minutes. Pour in 3 tablespoons of the simmering broth and cook for another 6–8 minutes. Add the spring onions. Season with salt.

Stir the cornflour mixture into the broth and cook until slightly thickened. Season to taste.

Meanwhile, bring a separate saucepan of water to the boil. Blanch the water spinach for 30 seconds, then transfer to a bowl of iced water. Repeat with the bean sprouts, placing them in a separate bowl. Season with salt.

Meanwhile, in a third saucepan, bring 1 litre/34 fl oz (4¼ cups) of water to the boil. Add the noodles and cook according to the package directions.

Drain the noodles, then divide among 4 bowls. Ladle the broth over each bowl and top with the sautéed mushrooms, water spinach and bean sprouts. Drizzle with sesame oil. Serve with crispy shallots, garlic chips, lime wedges and boiled sambal.

Savoy Cabbage, Miso and Coconut Parcels

Buntil Tauco

My mum was born and raised in Jakarta, and this was one of her favourite dishes growing up. Traditionally, it's made with cassava or papaya leaves and filled with dry salted fish or baby prawns (shrimp). For ease, I've used savoy cabbage and swapped in miso to keep that deep, umami flavour. The leafy parcels are simmered in a rich, spiced coconut milk broth with butter (lima) beans, creating a dish that's savoury, spicy and wonderfully creamy. The leaves cook down until soft and tender, almost melting into the sauce – the kind of comforting texture that lingers. It is best served warm with steamed rice.

Preparation time: 20 minutes
Cooking time: 40 minutes

Serves 4

For the coconut filling:
* 400 g/14 oz cavolo nero, stemmed and coarsely chopped
* 275 g/9¾ oz (3¼ cups) freshly grated coconut (see Note)
* 100 g/3½ oz (1 cup) fresh or frozen edamame, thawed if frozen
* 1 quantity White Spice Paste (page 32)
* 1 tablespoon miso paste
* salt, to taste

For the parcels:
* 4 large leaves savoy cabbage
* 1 (400-g/14-oz) can butter (lima) beans in water, drained
* salt and black pepper, to taste
* Steamed Black Rice (page 40), to serve (optional)

For the sauce:
* 2 tablespoons coconut oil or sunflower oil
* 400 ml/14 fl oz (1⅔ cups) coconut milk
* 6 green bird's eye chillies
* 3 bay leaves
* 3 makrut lime leaves
* 1 tablespoon ground coriander

To make the coconut filling, bring a saucepan of water to the boil. Add the cavolo nero, then drain. Set aside to cool slightly, then gently squeeze out the excess water.

Combine the grated coconut, edamame, half of the white spice paste and miso in a bowl. Season with salt and mix well.

To make the parcels, bring a large saucepan of water to the boil. Add the cabbage and cook for 2–3 minutes. Drain, then transfer the leaves into a large bowl of cold water. Drain again, carefully squeezing out the excess water. If desired, trim the thicker end of the leaves to make it easier to roll the parcel.

Spread out a cabbage leaf. Add 2 tablespoons of the coconut filling along the thicker end of the leaf. Roll the leaf tightly, tucking in the sides to enclose them. Place the parcels in a large saucepan, seam-side down, in a single layer. Repeat with the remaining cabbage leaves and filling. Set aside.

Next, make the sauce. Heat the oil in a frying pan over medium-high heat. Add the remaining white spice paste and cook for 3 minutes until fragrant. Pour in the coconut milk and 400 ml/14 fl oz (1⅔ cups) of water, then add the chillies, bay leaves, makrut lime leaves and coriander. Mix well.

Pour the sauce over the parcels and bring to the boil. Reduce the heat to medium-low and simmer uncovered for 25 minutes until very tender.

Add the beans and stir gently. Cook for another 10 minutes, until hot. Season to taste and serve with steamed rice.

Note: Freshly grated coconut can be substituted with 50 g/1¾ oz (scant ¾ cup) of unsweetened desiccated coconut soaked in 100 ml/3½ fl oz (scant ½ cup) of coconut milk. Soak for 20 minutes, then set aside.

Hearty Vegetables

Sayuran Yang Mengenyangkan

I grew up in the suburbs of Manado, North Sulawesi, where the earth was generous, offering an abundance of root vegetables and spices that shaped not only our meals but our daily rituals. My earliest memories are filled with the scent of boiling sweet potatoes or taro and fried cassava, served alongside ginger-infused tea or coffee.

My grandmother Oma Merey often served mashed cassava with freshly grated coconut and shaved palm sugar. I'd watch her peel cassava with the ease of someone who had done it for decades. She always preferred the yellow-fleshed cassava for its rich, buttery flavour over the white variety. In Java, cassava takes on yet another form: fermented, subtly sweet and tender (see page 207).

Oma's garden was full of fiery red-skinned spicy ginger (*jahe merah*), turmeric and galangal. It wasn't until I moved to Java that I discovered larger ginger varieties and sand ginger (*kencur*) – a small rhizome with a bold, unique aroma essential to Balinese and West Javanese cooking. As I travelled more across the archipelago, I came across even more root vegetables like arrowroot and lotus root, often grown in shallow ponds, as well as lesser-known rhizomes such as key ginger, Java ginger, white turmeric and a turmeric with mango-like notes. Many of these are used in *jamu*, the traditional Javanese practice of herbal wellness.

Today, root vegetables and spices once tied to specific places are found in markets across the world – including where I live in the UK – making it easier than ever to cook these dishes far from home. This global accessibility is a reminder of how food connects us. Every shared recipe becomes a bridge between past and present, between home and the world beyond.

In this book, I've also included recipes for celeriac (celery root), whose leaves remind me of *seledri* in Indonesia, where the foliage is used more than the root. You'll also find carrots, parsnips (known in Indonesia as 'white carrots'), daikon and potatoes – humble British ingredients that, like roots themselves, run deep with memory and meaning.

Crudités of the Archipelago

Lalapan Nusantara

Across the Indonesian archipelago, *lalapan* is more than a side dish – it's a raw, vibrant expression of freshness and local identity. Think of it as the Southeast Asian cousin to French crudités, served with bold sambals. I've swapped in some accessible vegetables for ease, but feel free to get creative.

Preparation time: 20 minutes
Cooking time: 10 minutes

Serves 10–12

- 12 baby carrots with tops
- 1 cucumber, cut into 10-cm/4-inch sticks
- 1 baby gem lettuce, leaves separated and halved lengthwise
- 1 red chicory (endive), leaves separated
- 1 pink chicory (endive), leaves separated
- 1 red bell pepper, seeded, deveined and sliced
- 20 vine-ripened cherry tomatoes
- 12 radishes, halved
- 12 baby corn
- 12 sugar snaps
- small bunch of basil
- edible flowers (optional)

For the tempeh and tofu:

- 2 cloves garlic, finely chopped
- 1 banana shallot, finely grated
- 1 tablespoon ground coriander
- 1 teaspoon salt
- 200 g/7 oz tempeh, cut into bite-size pieces
- 200 g/7 oz firm tofu, cut into triangles
- 400 ml/14 fl oz (1⅔ cups) sunflower oil

To serve:

- 1 quantity Smoked Tomato Sambal (page 36)
- 1 quantity Aubergine Sambal (page 33)
- 1 quantity Tahini Sambal (page 36)

Arrange the vegetables, basil and flowers, if using, on a platter and refrigerate until ready to serve.

To prepare the tempeh and tofu, mix the garlic, shallot, coriander and salt with 200 ml/7 fl oz (scant 1 cup) of water in a large bowl. Add the tempeh and tofu and set aside to marinate for 5 minutes.

Heat the oil in a frying pan over medium-high heat. Working in batches, add the tempeh and tofu and fry for 3–4 minutes on each side until golden. Drain on paper towels.

Serve the tofu and tempeh on top of the vegetables along with the sambals.

Celeriac, Spiced Tofu and Lemongrass Soto
Soto Tahu

This *soto* is a nourishing bowl of warmth, layered with deep, aromatic flavours. At its heart are tender celeriac (celery root) and tofu, nestled in a rich golden broth infused with turmeric, lemongrass and makrut lime leaves. The result is a vibrant, comforting dish – wholesome, satisfying and full of character. With its delicate balance of flavours and variety of textures, it's a meal that invites you to slow down and savour.

Preparation time: 20 minutes
Cooking time: 30 minutes

Serves 4

For the broth:
- 1 celeriac (celery root), peeled and quartered
- 4 cloves garlic, coarsely chopped
- 4 spring onions (scallions)
- 4 makrut lime leaves, torn in half
- 2 stalks lemongrass, crushed and tied into a knot
- 2 stalks celery, coarsely chopped
- 2 red bird's eye chillies
- 1 (10-cm/4-inch) piece of fresh root ginger, finely grated
- 1 (10-cm/4-inch) piece of fresh turmeric, finely grated
- 10 black peppercorns
- salt, to taste
- 200 g/7 oz Fresh Tofu (page 44), sliced into bite-size pieces
- 1 tablespoon lime juice

To serve:
- 80 g/2¾ oz glass noodles, soaked in hot water for 8–10 minutes
- 100 g/3½ oz cabbage, shredded
- 100 g/3½ oz (1 cup) bean sprouts, roots removed
- 2 tomatoes, seeded and diced
- 2 tablespoons chopped parsley
- 2 tablespoons Crispy Shallots (page 41)
- 1 tablespoon Garlic Chips (page 42), coarsely ground
- Boiled Sambal (page 34) (optional)
- lime wedges

In a large saucepan, combine the celeriac (celery root) and 1 litre/34 fl oz (4¼ cups) of room-temperature water. Add all the remaining broth ingredients except the tofu and lime juice. Season with salt. Bring to the boil, then reduce the heat to medium-low. Simmer for 30 minutes until the flavours are infused and the celeriac has softened.

Remove the pan from the heat. Transfer the celeriac to a plate and leave to cool slightly, then cut into bite-size pieces. Strain the liquid into a separate saucepan.

Add the celeriac pieces and tofu to the strained broth and bring to the boil. Simmer for 5–7 minutes. Season with salt and lime juice.

Drain the glass noodles and refresh with cold water. Drain.

Create a nest of glass noodles in each serving bowl. Add the celeriac, tofu, cabbage, bean sprouts and tomatoes among them. Sprinkle with parsley. Pour 2 ladlefuls of hot broth into each bowl and sprinkle with crispy shallots and garlic chips. Serve immediately with sambal, if using, and lime wedges.

Roasted Sweet Potato Soup with Ginger and Coconut Milk

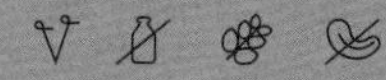

Sup Ubi Manis Panggang dengan Jahe dan Santan

This dish reminds me of my Oma's (grandmother's) simple yet delicious home cooking. The fragrant mix of ginger, garlic, sweet potato and coconut milk captures the essence of my region's authentic flavours.

I prefer to roast the sweet potato first to deepen its flavour, and while the Manadonese typically use shallots, I use onion for its convenience.

Preparation time: 15 minutes
Cooking time: 50–55 minutes

Serves 6–8

* 3 sweet potatoes, peeled and sliced into 3-cm/1¼-inch cubes
* 1–1½ teaspoons salt
* 3 tablespoons coconut oil or vegetable oil
* 3 cloves garlic, finely chopped
* 1 onion, finely chopped
* 20 g/¾ oz fresh root ginger, finely grated
* 400 ml/14 fl oz (1⅔ cups) coconut milk
* black pepper, to taste

Preheat the oven to 180°C/350°F/Gas Mark 4. Line a baking sheet with baking (parchment) paper.

Place the sweet potatoes on the prepared baking sheet. Season with ½ teaspoon of the salt and 2 tablespoons of the oil. Using your hands, mix to coat. Roast for 30–35 minutes until tender. Set aside.

Heat the remaining tablespoon of oil in a large saucepan over medium heat. Add the garlic and onion and sauté for 5 minutes, until softened but not coloured. Add the ginger and sauté for another minute. Stir in the sweet potatoes and cook for 2 minutes, then pour in most of the coconut milk (reserving 4–6 tablespoons for drizzling) and 350 ml/12 fl oz (1½ cups) of hot water. Bring to the boil, then reduce the heat to medium-low and simmer for 5 minutes.

Season the mixture with the remaining ½–1 teaspoon of salt and some pepper. Using an immersion blender, blend until smooth. Bring the soup to the boil, then simmer for 8 minutes until piping hot. Check the seasoning.

Ladle the soup into bowls and drizzle each with 1 tablespoon of the reserved coconut milk.

Leftover soup can be stored in the freezer for 2 weeks.

Beetroot Salad with Pineapple Sambal

Selada Bit dan Sambal Nanas

I love the vivid colour and health benefits of beetroots (beets). Its deep, earthy sweetness forms a lush, velvety base that pairs beautifully with the sharp, tangy heat of pineapple sambal. The sambal's natural sugar and spicy kick cut through the beetroot's richness, adding nuance. A mix of fresh baby salad leaves – slightly bitter and peppery – offers a crisp contrast, enhancing the interplay of flavours. The result is a striking dish that unites sweet, fiery and fresh notes, awakening the palate with every bite.

Preparation time: 10 minutes
Cooking time: 25 minutes

Serves 4

* 500 g/1 lb 2 oz baby beetroots (beets), rinsed well
* 1 quantity Pineapple Sambal (page 35)
* salt, to taste
* 1 (125-g/4¼-oz) pack baby salad leaves
* 2 tablespoons mixed seeds, such as sunflower, pumpkin and chia

Place the beetroots (beets) in a saucepan and add enough water to submerge them. Bring to the boil, then reduce the heat to medium-low and simmer for 25 minutes until tender.

Drain the beetroots and when cool enough to handle, rub off the skins with your fingers. Cut the beetroots into wedges.

Place the beetroot wedges in a bowl, add the sambal and season with salt. Add the salad leaves and seeds and toss lightly. Serve.

Steamed Plantain and Root Vegetables

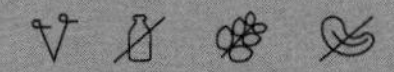

Pisang Tanduk Kukus dan Beragam Umbi-umbian

Before rice became Indonesia's daily staple, people nourished themselves with roots, tubers and plantains – foods grown close to the earth, steamed simply and eaten with sambal, grated coconut or palm sugar. I remember my grandmother eating these with joy. Although humble, they carry cultural and ceremonial significance. Today, they are being rediscovered as wholesome, sustainable alternatives for the modern table.

Preparation time: 10 minutes
Cooking time: 1 hour

Serves 4–6

* 4 small taros
* 1 large cassava, peeled and cut into 4–6 pieces
* 2 sweet potatoes, unpeeled, cut into 3–4 pieces
* 1 ripe yellow plantain, unpeeled, cut into 4 pieces

To serve:
* Green Sambal (page 34)
* Smoked Tomato Sambal (page 36)
* Almond Sambal (page 33)

Place the taros and cassava in a large steamer and steam for 30 minutes.

Add the sweet potatoes and plantain to the steamer and steam for another 30 minutes, until all are soft and tender.

Serve warm with the sambals.

Spiced Whole Cauliflower in Banana Leaf

Pepes Kembang Kol Utuh

Bring Indonesian flavours into your kitchen by transforming a simple cauliflower into a showstopper, coating it in a fragrant blend of aromatics, wrapping it in banana leaves and slow-roasting it until tender and infused with deep earthy spices. Inspired by a traditional cooking method known as *pepes*, this technique locks in moisture and adds a subtle aroma. I find its golden hue and rich scent evoke the vibrant markets of Indonesia.

Serve with a *dabu-dabu* sambal mixed with avocado – the freshness of tomatoes, creamy avocado and herbs balances the bold spices.

Preparation time: 10 minutes
Cooking time: 1 hour

Serves 4–6

For the cauliflower:
* 1 (650-g/1 lb 7-oz) cauliflower, stalk trimmed
* 1 teaspoon salt
* 1 tablespoon coconut oil
* 1 quantity Yellow Spice Paste (page 32)
* 1 banana leaf, cut into 4 (60-cm/2-ft) lengths, wiped clean
* small bunch of basil, chopped, to garnish

For the tomato-avocado salsa:
* 2 avocados, stoned and chopped
* 1 quantity Chilli and Tomato Sambal (page 34)

Preheat the oven to 220°C/425°F/Gas Mark 7.

Soak the whole cauliflower in boiling water for 10 minutes. Drain cauliflower, then set aside to cool.

Mix the salt, coconut oil and half of the spice paste. Rub the mixture over the cauliflower.

Place 2 layers of banana leaves (or baking paper) on a clean, dry surface. Place the cauliflower at one edge of the banana leaf and roll it up. Secure both sides by folding down the edges. Put the parcel, head up, on a baking sheet and roast for 1 hour until cooked through. Remove from the oven.

Meanwhile, make the salsa by combining both ingredients in a bowl.

Remove the top of the banana leaves using a knife or scissors. Using tongs, carefully transfer the cauliflower to a serving plate. Using a large spoon, scoop the paste and the liquid from the tray and baste the cauliflower. Spoon the salsa around the base and sprinkle with basil. Slice the cauliflower and serve.

Roasted Vegetables with Two Sambals

Beragam Sayur Panggang dengan Dua Sambal

In this recipe, a combination of sambals transforms even the simplest roasted vegetables into a dish full of character and warmth.

Shallot sambal is one of the simplest yet most essential condiments in Indonesian cooking. Made with shallots, garlic and chillies, it's a bold, aromatic sambal that enhances just about anything. I use it throughout this book as an easy, authentic way to add Indonesian flavour.

The other is *pili sambal*, made with pili nuts *{kacang kanari)*, often called Indonesia's answer to almonds. These nuts give the sambal a rich, creamy texture and a luxurious feel. A delicacy from Banda Island, pili sambal can be hard to source, so I often make an almond version that's just as satisfying.

Preparation time: 15 minutes
Cooking time: 35–40 minutes

Serves 6–8

* 1 small pumpkin, cut into 12–16 wedges, unpeeled
* 2 aubergines (eggplants), cut into 2-cm/¾-inch-thick discs
* 1 quantity Shallot Sambal (page 36)
* salt and black pepper, to taste
* 4 tablespoons coconut oil or sunflower oil
* 1 sweetheart cabbage, cut lengthwise into 6–8 wedges
* 2 vine-ripened tomatoes
* 1 quantity Almond Sambal (page 33), to serve

Preheat the oven to 200°C/400°F/Gas Mark 6.

Brush the pumpkin and aubergine (eggplant) slices with shallot sambal, then season with salt and pepper. Drizzle with 3 tablespoons of the sunflower oil and toss well. Spread out on a baking sheet, skin-side down for the pumpkin, and roast for 20 minutes.

Add the cabbage and tomatoes to the baking sheet, season with salt and pepper and drizzle with the final tablespoon of sunflower oil. Roast for 15–20 minutes, until the vegetables are cooked through and slightly coloured.

Meanwhile, make the sambal. Spread the almonds over a baking sheet and roast on the lowest shelf of the oven for 8–10 minutes, until golden.

Heat the coconut oil in a saucepan over medium heat. Add the garlic and shallot and sauté for 2–3 minutes until fragrant. Add the chillies and sauté for another 2–3 minutes. Remove from the heat.

In a blender, combine the almonds, shallot-chilli mixture and 200 ml/7 fl oz (scant 1 cup) of water and blend until thick and smooth. If necessary, add a little more water. Transfer to a bowl, then add the lime juice and white pepper and season with salt.

To serve, spread the vegetables over a large serving platter and drizzle with the sambal.

Fried Cassava with Miso Sambal

Singkong Goreng dengan Sambal Tauco

Fried cassava with sambal is golden and crisp on the outside, soft and almost creamy within – a contrast that makes it especially satisfying. I like to parboil the cassava first with garlic and turmeric for extra depth of flavour. Made from the most basic ingredients, it's a humble dish that carries the warmth of home, the echo of laughter and childhood moments spent in the kitchen, eagerly awaiting the first bite.

These days, fried cassava and sambal even appear in five-star establishments in Jakarta. I once enjoyed it at afternoon tea with a friend and was delighted. Still, one bite takes me back – barefoot in my grandmother's kitchen, eyes wide with anticipation, savouring the comfort of something so familiar.

Preparation time: 10 minutes
Cooking time: 40–45 minutes

Serves 6–8

- 3 cloves garlic, thinly sliced
- 1 kg/2 lbs 4 oz cassava
- 1 teaspoon ground turmeric (optional)
- 1 teaspoon salt
- sunflower oil, for deep-frying

For the miso sambal:

- 2 tablespoons coconut oil or sunflower oil
- 2 banana shallots, finely chopped
- 2 large red chillies, finely chopped
- 2–4 red bird's eye chillies, coarsely chopped
- 2 tablespoons light or dark miso paste
- 1 tablespoon honey
- salt, to taste

Bring a saucepan of water to the boil. Add the garlic, cassava, turmeric, if using, and salt. Boil for 15–20 minutes, until the cassava has softened but is not falling apart. Drain, then set aside to cool.

To make the miso sambal, heat the oil in a frying pan over medium heat. Add the shallots and sauté for 3–4 minutes until softened. Add the chillies and sauté for another 1–2 minutes. Stir in the miso, honey and 3½ tablespoons of water. Bring to the boil, then simmer for 5–7 minutes. Set aside to cool.

When cool, transfer the miso mixture to a blender and blend until smooth. Season with salt.

Heat the oil for deep-frying in a deep saucepan over medium heat. The oil is ready when a cube of bread dropped in sizzles on contact and turns golden in 10–15 seconds. (Alternatively, use a thermometer and heat to 180°C/350°F.)

Cut the cassava into chunky sticks. Gently lower 4–6 pieces into the oil and deep-fry for 5–7 minutes on each side, until golden brown. Transfer to a plate lined with paper towels to drain. Repeat with the remaining sticks.

Serve hot with the sambal.

Variation:
Sprinkle grated mature Cheddar cheese on the hot cassava before serving. Remember to check if the cheese is vegetarian-friendly, as traditional Cheddar uses animal rennet.

Roasted Parsnips, Carrots and Brussels Sprouts with Tahini Sambal

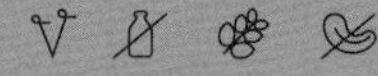

Wortel Putih, Wortel, dan Ceriwis Panggang dengan Sambal Wijen Putih

Cooking root vegetables like carrots and parsnips with Brussels sprouts is essential in my kitchen during celebrations – these are my husband's favourites. In Indonesia, we have a similar vegetable to Brussels sprouts, from the same cruciferous family but with a longer, oval shape and looser leaves. The earthy sweetness of the roots pairs with the sprouts' slight bitterness for a harmonious mix of flavours and textures. Served with rich tahini sambal, the dish comes to life: creamy, nutty tahini balances the vegetables, while the sambal adds a zesty, spicy kick. It's a comforting combination of warmth, depth and spice – perfect alongside Spiced Tempeh and Mushroom Stew (page 84).

Preparation time: 15 minutes
Cooking time: 35–40 minutes

Serves 6

* 3–4 parsnips, halved lengthwise
* 5 small carrots, halved lengthwise
* 1 quantity Tahini Sambal (page 36)
* salt, to taste
* 250 g/9 oz Brussels sprouts, halved
* black pepper, to taste
* 3 tablespoons sunflower oil
* 6 spring onions (scallions), thinly sliced diagonally
* 2 tablespoons sesame seeds, toasted

Preheat the oven to 190°C/375°F/Gas Mark 5.

Bring a large saucepan of salted water to the boil. Add the parsnips and carrots and cook for 5 minutes. Drain, then place in a roasting pan. Add the Brussels sprouts. Season with salt and pepper.

Combine the sambal with 3 tablespoons of water. Mix well and season with salt. Add a little more water, if necessary.

Place the mixture over the vegetables and toss well. Drizzle with the sunflower oil.

Roast for 30–35 minutes, turning halfway through, until everything is golden brown and caramelised.

Transfer the roasted vegetables to a large platter. Sprinkle with the spring onions (scallions) and toasted sesame seeds, then serve.

Spiced Coconut Omelette in Ginger-turmeric Broth

Telur Dadar Serundeng dengan Kuah Jahe dan Kunyit

This dish is inspired *kerak telur,* the classic Jakarta omelette and iconic Betawi street snack that's becoming harder to find. Traditionally cooked in a small wok over a charcoal fire without oil, soaked sticky rice is spread in the pan, then topped with egg and seasonings. Once set, the wok is flipped over the flame, giving the omelette its crispy, slightly charred edges. My version keeps most of the original ingredients but uses the coconut differently. Savoury dried coconut, crispy shallots, bean sprouts and celery leaves add freshness and crunch, while a warm ginger–turmeric broth makes it a cozy winter breakfast.

Preparation time: 20 minutes
Cooking time: 35 minutes

Serves 2

For the ginger-turmeric broth:
* 50 g/1¾ oz fresh root ginger, thinly sliced
* 30 g/1 oz fresh turmeric, thinly sliced
* salt and white pepper, to taste

For the spiced coconut:
* 2 tablespoons coconut oil
* 2 cloves garlic, finely chopped
* 10 g/¼ oz fresh root ginger, grated
* 10 g/¼ oz galangal, finely grated (optional)
* 2 red bird's eye chillies, finely chopped
* 10 g/¼ oz turmeric, finely grated
* 100 g/3½ oz (1¼ cups) unsweetened desiccated coconut
* 2 tablespoons Crispy Shallots (page 41)

For the omelette:
* 4 eggs
* salt, to taste
* 1 tablespoon coconut oil
* 50 g/1¾ oz (½ cup) bean sprouts, roots removed
* small bunch of celery leaves or parsley, finely chopped
* 2 tablespoons Crispy Shallots (page 41)

First, make the ginger-turmeric broth. In a saucepan, combine the ginger, turmeric and 600 ml/20 fl oz (2½ cups) of water. Bring to the boil, then reduce the heat to medium and simmer for 30 minutes to infuse. Season with a little salt and pepper. Set aside.

Meanwhile, make the spiced coconut. Heat the oil in a frying pan over medium-high heat. Add the garlic, ginger, galangal, if using, chillies and turmeric and sauté for 4 minutes until fragrant. Add the coconut and sauté for 10 minutes, stirring constantly. Sprinkle with the crispy shallots and set aside to cool.

Transfer the spiced coconut to an airtight container. It will keep in the refrigerator for up to 1 week or in the freezer for up to 1 month. Bring to room temperature or gently reheat in a dry pan before serving, to refresh the texture.

For the omelette, combine the eggs and 2 tablespoons of the spiced coconut in a small bowl and beat gently. Season with salt.

Heat ½ tablespoon of the coconut oil in a small frying pan over medium heat. Pour the egg mixture into the pan and tilt the pan to create an omelette in a half-moon shape in the lower half of the pan. Keep folding the egg mixture for 1–2 minutes until set, then roll the omelette sideways to cook the reverse side for another 30 seconds. Transfer the cooked omelette to a plate lined with a paper towel.

Repeat to cook the second omelette.

To serve, place each omelette in a shallow bowl and ladle over the warm broth. Top with the bean sprouts, celery leaves and crispy shallots.

Pasta and Sambal Matah

Pasta dan Sambal Matah

This dish reimagines classic flavours with *sambal matah* – Bali's vibrant raw sambal made with lemongrass, chillies, makrut lime leaves, and, when available, ginger flowers. The result is a pasta bowl full of umami, heat and brightness.

Quick to prepare yet full of character, it's impressive enough for guests – an easy dish that delivers far more than the sum of its parts.

Preparation time: 15 minutes
Cooking time: 15 minutes

Serves 4

* 350 g/12 oz spaghetti
* 2 tablespoons extra-virgin coconut oil
* juice of 2 limes
* salt and black pepper, to taste

For the sambal matah:

* 5 makrut lime leaves, centre stem removed and thinly sliced
* 3 stalks lemongrass, white part only, thinly sliced
* 2–3 heaped tablespoons extra-virgin coconut oil
* 2 banana shallots, thinly sliced
* 1–2 red bird's eye chillies, finely chopped
* 2 large red chillies, finely chopped
* 2 pink ginger flower buds, thinly sliced (optional)
* salt, to taste

To make the sambal matah, combine all the ingredients in a bowl. Set aside.

Cook the pasta in a saucepan of salted boiling water, according to the package instructions, until al dente. Drain, reserving 100 ml/3½ fl oz (scant ½ cup) of the pasta cooking water.

Heat 1 tablespoon of the coconut oil in a pan over medium heat. Add the sambal matah and cook for 1 minute. Stir in the pasta and toss well, adding the reserved pasta water to create a light sauce.

Remove from the heat, stir in the lime juice and remaining coconut oil and season with salt and pepper. Serve.

Variations:

- **Courgette Noodles with Sambal Matah**
  This gluten-free version replaces the pasta with fresh courgette (zucchini) noodles. The delicate texture and mild sweetness pair nicely with the sambal's vibrant heat.

  * 4 courgettes (zucchini), spiralised into noodles
  * salt and black pepper
  * 1 tablespoon coconut oil
  * 1 quantity Sambal Matah (see above)

  Toss the courgette (zucchini) noodles with a pinch of salt. Heat 1 tablespoon of oil in a frying pan over medium heat. Add the courgette noodles and sauté for 2 minutes until just tender. Add the sambal and toss to coat. Loosen with a splash of water if needed. Season to taste and serve.

- **Pasta with Sambal Lu'at**
  Here, the fiery intensity of the sambal is tempered by bright citrus notes and fragrant, lemon-scented basil traditionally used in the region of Flores. I've substituted the local *kemangi* basil with common basil, which still harmonises beautifully with the dish's layered flavours.

  * 4 red bird's eye chillies, finely chopped
  * 3 large red chillies, finely chopped
  * 2 banana shallots, finely chopped
  * small bunch of basil, coarsely chopped
  * ½ teaspoon salt
  * ½ teaspoon sugar (optional)
  * zest and juice of 2 lemons
  * peel of 1 lemon (zest + pith), finely chopped

  Using a pestle and mortar, grind the chillies to release the juices. Combine all the ingredients in a bowl, then season to taste. Transfer to a jar and refrigerate.

  The sambal can be stored for up to 10 days in the refrigerator and the flavours will deepen with time.

Mushrooms

Jamur

Native mushrooms grow across the archipelago's diverse landscapes – from the cool highlands of Papua to the rainforests of Sumatra – offering a range of textures, flavours and medicinal uses. Yet many remain difficult to access beyond their regions of origin. The only truly endemic one I've tasted is *jamur pelawan* from Bangka Island, an experience that only deepened my desire to explore more.

Straw mushrooms are among the most widely cultivated, grown on rice straw as a natural medium. They start as small, egg-shaped buttons before unfurling into umbrella-like caps. Mild and slightly sweet, they're lighter than shiitake and ideal for stir-fries or soups. Wood ear mushrooms are another favourite. Their curious shape and slippery crunch made them a comforting addition to my mum's *kimlo*, a light vegetable and glass noodle soup (shared in my first book, *The Indonesian Table*).

Markets in cities with strong Chinese-Indonesian communities often carry fresh mushrooms like wood ear and shiitake, reflecting the lasting influence of Chinese traditions in Indonesian cooking.

What draws me to mushrooms is how grounding they feel. Their earthy, damp scent recalls forest floors and rain-soaked soil, and each variety has its own character – the jelly-like crunch of wood ear, the tender bite of straw mushrooms, the deep umami they release when cooked. It's easy to see why they've long been valued for both nourishment and healing.

That sense of wonder is echoed at Locavore NXT in Ubud, Bali, where one of the most impressive mushroom farms I've visited thrives. Inside their climate-controlled indoor facility – essential in Bali's 35°C (95°F) heat – nearly 30 varieties grow, creating an environment that feels almost otherworldly.

Today, Asian mushrooms are widely available worldwide. In the UK, supermarkets and Asian food stores often stock fresh shiitake, oyster and dried wood ear, making it simple to bring Indonesian flavours into daily meals. Wild native varieties, however, remain rare outside Indonesia. I hope to experience more of them one day, in the forests and regional kitchens where they are still part of daily life.

Mushroom and Coconut Soup
Sup Jamur dengan Santan

This vegan dish isn't traditionally Indonesian, but it captures the essence of our flavours beautifully. The earthiness of mushrooms, the citrussy aroma of makrut lime leaves and the gentle warmth of lemongrass come together to create a deeply comforting and aromatic soup. Coconut milk adds a velvety richness.

Preparation time: 15 minutes, plus 20–30 minutes soaking time
Cooking time: 40–50 minutes

Serves 4

- 25 g/1 oz dried shiitake or porcini mushrooms
- 2 tablespoons coconut oil
- 2 large banana shallots, minced
- 3 cloves garlic, minced
- 2 bay leaves
- 300 g/10½ oz assorted mushrooms, such as oyster, button and shiitake, coarsely chopped
- 1 stalk lemongrass, crushed and tied in a knot
- 6 makrut lime leaves, torn
- 1 potato, finely diced
- 1 teaspoon salt
- 1 teaspoon white pepper
- 400 ml/14 fl oz (1⅔ cups) coconut milk

For the topping:
- 4 tablespoons coconut milk
- pinch of chilli powder

Soak the dried mushrooms in hot water for 20–30 minutes to soften. Drain, reserving the soaking water.

Heat the coconut oil in a frying pan over medium heat. Add the shallots, garlic and bay leaves and cook for 8 minutes, until the shallots are translucent. Add the fresh mushrooms, lemongrass and makrut lime leaves and cook for 10 minutes, until mushrooms are tender and any moisture has evaporated. Add the potato, rehydrated mushrooms, salt and pepper and cook for 3 minutes.

Pour in half of the coconut milk and the reserved soaking liquid and simmer for 2–3 minutes, until the mushrooms have absorbed the coconut milk. Add 200 ml/7 fl oz (scant 1 cup) of water and bring to the boil. Reduce the heat to low, cover and cook for 20–30 minutes.

Add the remaining coconut milk and discard the lemongrass, makrut lime leaves and bay leaves. Using an immersion blender, blend the mixture until smooth.

Serve the soup in small bowls. Drizzle with coconut milk and sprinkle with chilli powder.

Stir-fried Shiitake Mushrooms and Sugar Snaps
Tumis Jamur Shiitake dan Kapri Manis

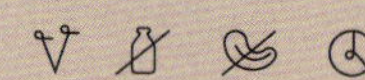

A handful of fresh ingredients, a hot wok or frying pan and just the right balance of seasoning can create something magical. This stir-fry is exactly that – quick, humble and bursting with flavour and texture. The earthy, meaty mushrooms soak up the savoury sauce, while the snap peas add a bright, sweet crunch. A perfect harmony of softness and crispness, this dish needs little more than steamed red rice or noodles on the side.

Preparation time: 10 minutes
Cooking time: 10–15 minutes

Serves 4–6

- 2 tablespoons vegetable oil
- 2 banana shallots, thinly sliced
- 3 cloves garlic, finely chopped
- 1 large red chilli, thinly sliced
- 1 red bird's eye chilli, thinly sliced, or 1 teaspoon crushed chilli flakes
- 3 tablespoons light soy sauce
- 10–12 shiitake mushrooms
- 200 g/7 oz sugar snap peas, trimmed
- pinch of sugar
- salt, to taste

Heat a wok or frying pan over high heat. Add the oil, shallots and garlic and sauté for 2–3 minutes until golden and fragrant. Add the chillies, soy sauce and mushrooms and stir-fry for 5–7 minutes, until the mushrooms soften. Add 3–4 tablespoons of water if the mixture is dry.

Stir in the sugar snaps and cook for another 2–3 minutes. Season with sugar and salt.

Serve immediately.

Baked Spring Rolls
Lumpia Panggang

Spring rolls come in countless regional varieties across the archipelago, each with its own twist. The most iconic are fresh or deep-fried *lumpia Semarang* from Central Java, filled with bamboo shoots, chicken or sometimes prawn (shrimp) and served with a thick, sweet-savoury sauce. In Bandung, *lumpia basah* offers a lighter, fresher take: a soft wrapper filled with stir-fried jicama, bean sprouts and egg. In Manado, where I spent part of my childhood, I adored *popiah* – fresh rolls of carrots and bamboo shoots served with spicy tomato sauce.

Growing up in Jakarta, I always enjoyed *lumpia goreng* as a treat: crispy, golden and stuffed with vermicelli and vegetables. I still remember the joy of biting into one hot from a street stall fryer, dipped in sambal – the crunch, the warmth of the filling, the pure pleasure of it. This version takes inspiration from those fried rolls, using mushrooms and filo (phyllo) pastry, but baked for ease.

Preparation time: 20 minutes
Cooking time: 30–35 minutes

Serves 7

* 1 (270-g) pack filo (phyllo) pastry sheets
* 4 tablespoons butter, melted
* 2 tablespoons sunflower oil
* Sriracha, to serve

For the filling:

* 2 tablespoons sunflower oil
* 2 banana shallots, finely sliced
* 150 g/5½ oz shiitake mushrooms, finely chopped
* 150 g/5½ oz Portobello mushrooms, finely chopped
* 3 tablespoons soy sauce
* ½ teaspoon salt
* 1 tablespoon white pepper
* 1 tablespoon cornflour (cornstarch)
* 1 large carrot, grated
* 3 spring onions (scallions), thinly sliced

First, make the filling. Heat the oil in a large frying pan over medium heat. Add the shallots and sauté for 4–5 minutes until soft. Increase the heat, add the mushrooms and cook for 10 minutes, until the mushrooms have softened and the water has evaporated. Season with soy sauce, salt and pepper and cook for another 2 minutes. Transfer to a bowl.

Sprinkle the cornflour (cornstarch) over the mushroom mixture and mix well, then stir in the carrot and spring onions (scallions) until combined. Set aside.

Preheat the oven to 200°C/400°F/Gas Mark 6.

Put the pastry sheets on a chopping (cutting) board and cut them in half to create 14 squares. Cover them with a clean dish towel to prevent them drying out.

Place 2–3 heaped tablespoons of the filling in the middle of each pastry square. Brush all 4 edges with melted butter and roll up into a cigar shape, tucking in the sides to seal. Place on a baking sheet. Repeat with the remaining filo (phyllo) and filling.

Brush the spring rolls with oil and bake for 12–15 minutes, turning halfway through, until golden and crispy.

Arrange on a platter and serve with Sriracha.

Variation:

- **Deep-Fried Spring Rolls**
  Use spring roll pastry instead of filo. Make the rolls as instructed above. Heat 250 ml/8 fl oz (1 cup) of oil in a deep pan or wok to 180°C (350°F). Carefully lower a few spring rolls into the hot oil and deep-fry for 4–5 minutes, turning them frequently, until golden. Transfer to a plate lined with paper towels to drain. Serve hot with Sriracha.

Stir-fried Noodles with Mushrooms and Pak Choy

Mie Goreng dengan Jamur dan Sawi

Mie goreng is one of Indonesia's most iconic dishes. It's often cooked to order by street vendors, making each plate a personalised experience and a joyful ritual.

I love the dish with mushrooms. Egg noodles are tossed in garlic oil, soy sauce and white pepper, then combined with tender mushrooms and infused with sweet soy and herbs. This version bursts with flavour, thanks to the mushrooms' natural umami.

Preparation time: 15 minutes
Cooking time: 15 minutes

Serves 4–6

- 2 tablespoons sunflower oil
- 2 banana shallots, thinly sliced
- 4 cloves garlic, finely chopped
- 200 g/7 oz (2 cups) button (white) mushrooms, chopped into small chunks
- 100 g/3½ oz shiitake mushrooms, quartered
- 100 g/3½ oz oyster mushrooms, torn
- 500 g/1 lb 2 oz fresh egg noodles
- 5 tablespoons Sweet Soy Sauce (page 38)
- 4 tablespoons light soy sauce
- salt and white pepper, to taste
- 175 g/6 oz pak choy or chard, rinsed and cut into 5-mm/¼-inch lengths

To serve:

- 2 tablespoons finely chopped spring onions (scallions)
- 2 tablespoons finely chopped celery or parsley leaves
- 2 tablespoons Crispy Shallots (page 41)
- Pickled Pineapple (page 48) (optional)
- 2 tablespoons Sriracha

Heat the oil in a frying pan or wok over medium-high heat. Add the shallots and garlic and sauté for 3–4 minutes, then add the mushrooms, season with salt and sauté for 5–6 minutes, until softened. Add the fresh noodles and both soy sauces, toss and cook for another 3–4 minutes over high heat. Season with salt and pepper, then add the pak choy and sauté for a final minute.

Transfer the noodles to a large platter and sprinkle with the spring onions (scallions), celery leaves and crispy shallots. Serve with pickled pineapple, if using, and Sriracha.

Spicy Noodle Soup with Mushroom, Cabbage and Pak Choy

Mie Gomak Kuah

After more than 30 years, I returned to Lake Toba in North Sumatra and was captivated once again by its tranquil beauty. I stayed with my dear friend Dumasi in Dolok Sanggul, a charming village just 20 minutes from her lakeside garden, which even boasts water sports facilities. To my delight, Dumasi had arranged for a group of local women to cook for us. Among the many exquisite dishes, I had the pleasure of trying *gomak* noodles for the first time.

A Batak speciality, often referred to as 'Batak spaghetti', the dish features thick, chewy, hand-stretched noodles, gently cooked in a rich, aromatic coconut milk sauce, served either dry *(goreng)* or soupy *(kuah)* and beautifully flavoured with *andaliman*, a local peppercorn that imparts a numbing, citrussy heat reminiscent of Szechuan pepper. It is traditionally accompanied by crispy fried shallots, boiled eggs and fiery *tuktuk sambal*.

Preparation time: 15 minutes
Cooking time: 25–30 minutes

Serves 4

- 2 tablespoons coconut oil or sunflower oil
- 12–15 shiitake mushrooms
- 100 g/3½ oz cabbage, thinly sliced
- 2 pak choy
- 400 ml/14 fl oz (1⅔ cups) coconut milk
- 1 tablespoon lime juice
- 400 g/14 oz thick egg noodles
- salt, to taste
- pinch of ground Szechuan pepper, to taste
- Crispy Shallots, to garnish (page 41)

For the paste:

- 4 cloves garlic, sliced
- 2–3 small banana shallots, sliced
- 2–3 red bird's eye chillies, coarsely chopped
- 2 candlenuts or macadamia nuts, coarsely ground (optional)
- 2 large red chillies, coarsely chopped
- 7 g/¼ oz fresh turmeric, thinly sliced, or 1–1½ teaspoons ground turmeric
- 10 g/¼ oz fresh root ginger, thinly sliced

For the tuktuk sambal:

- 3 tablespoons coconut oil
- 2 banana shallots, finely chopped
- 3 cloves garlic, finely chopped
- 2 large chillies, finely chopped
- 2–3 red bird's eye chillies, finely chopped
- 2 candlenuts or macadamia nuts (optional)
- 10 g/¼ oz fresh root ginger, grated
- 1 small ginger flower bud, finely chopped
- 1 (10-cm/4-inch) ginger flower stem, finely chopped
- 1 tablespoon fresh andaliman or 1 teaspoon ground Szechuan pepper
- salt, to taste

First, make the paste. Combine all the ingredients in a small blender and blend well. Set aside.

Next, make the sambal. Heat the oil in a frying pan over medium heat. Add the shallots and garlic and sauté for 2–3 minutes, then chillies, candlenuts, fresh ginger and ginger flower bud. Cook for 4–5 minutes.

Add the ginger flower stem (reserving a little for garnish) and andaliman and season with salt. Set aside to cool.

Heat the oil in a wok or frying pan over medium heat. Add the paste and cook for 4–6 minutes, then add the mushrooms and cook for 6 minutes. Add the cabbage, pak choy, coconut milk and lime juice, bring to the boil, then reduce the heat to medium and simmer for 5 minutes. Add the noodles and cook for another 3 minutes. Season with salt and pepper.

Ladle into bowls, top with the crispy shallots and sambal and sprinkle with reserved ginger flower. Serve.

Mushroom Noodles with Tofu Dumplings

Bakmi Jakarta dengan Pangsit Tahu

The iconic *bakmi Jakarta* epitomises Jakarta's street food culture. Springy egg noodles are often topped with savoury chicken and mushrooms and served alongside a bowl of clear, fragrant broth. Omitting the chicken here doesn't take away from the comforting appeal – richly seasoned mushrooms more than hold their own. A crispy tofu wonton adds contrast, while a spoonful of sambal brings a spicy kick.

Preparation time: 40 minutes
Cooking time: 40 minutes

Serves 4

For the tofu dumplings:
* 200 g/7 oz Fresh Tofu (page 44), mashed
* 3 spring onions (scallions), thinly sliced
* 2 tablespoons sesame oil
* 2 tablespoons cornflour (cornstarch)
* 10 g/¼ oz fresh root ginger, finely grated
* 1 teaspoon white pepper
* 1 egg, lightly beaten
* ½ teaspoon salt
* 12 wonton wrappers
* 300 ml/10 fl oz (1¼ cups) sunflower oil, for deep-frying

For the garlic broth:
* 1 tablespoon vegetable oil
* 2 cloves garlic, finely chopped
* 2 spring onions (scallions), thinly sliced
* 1 tablespoon lime juice
* 1 teaspoon sugar
* 1 teaspoon white pepper
* salt, to taste

For the garlic oil:
* 100 ml/3½ fl oz (scant ½ cup) vegetable oil
* 6 cloves garlic, finely chopped
* salt, to taste

For the mushrooms:
* 3 tablespoons sunflower oil
* 1 banana shallot, thinly sliced
* 4 cloves garlic, finely chopped
* 400 g/14 oz shiitake or Portobello mushrooms, cut into bite-size pieces
* 3 makrut lime leaves, torn
* 2 salam leaves or bay leaves
* 1 stalk lemongrass, crushed and tied into a knot
* 10 g/¼ oz galangal, finely grated
* 5 tablespoons Sweet Soy Sauce (page 38)
* 2 tablespoons light soy sauce
* salt and white pepper, to taste

For the noodles:
* 400 g/14 oz fresh egg noodles or 300 g/10½ oz dried noodles
* 2 pak choy, cut into 1-cm/½-inch slices
* 4 teaspoons light soy sauce

To serve:
* 2 tablespoons finely chopped spring onions (scallions)
* Vinegar Sambal (page 34)

First, make the dumplings. Combine all the ingredients except the wonton wrappers and sunflower oil in a bowl. Place a teaspoon of the filling mixture off-centre in a wonton wrapper, fold into a triangle, then bring the two longer tips together and seal with water. Repeat to make 12 dumplings. Set aside.

Next, make the garlic broth. Heat the vegetable oil in a saucepan over medium heat. Add the garlic and sauté for 1 minute until fragrant. Add the remaining ingredients and 600 ml/20 fl oz (2½ cups) of water. Simmer for 5 minutes, then strain. Set aside.

To make the garlic oil, heat the oil in a small saucepan over medium-low heat. Add the garlic and sauté for 5 minutes until fragrant. Season with salt, then leave to cool.

Now prepare the mushrooms. Heat the sunflower oil in a small saucepan over medium-low heat. Add the shallot and garlic and cook for 3–4 minutes, then add the mushrooms, makrut lime leaves, salam leaves, lemongrass and galangal. Cook for 10 minutes. Add both soy sauces and 3 tablespoons of water and simmer for another 10 minutes. Discard the herbs and season to taste.

Heat the oil for deep-frying in a deep saucepan or wok over medium heat. The oil is ready when a cube of bread dropped in sizzles on contact and turns golden in 10–15 seconds. (Alternatively, use a thermometer and heat to 180°C/350°F.)

Carefully lower the dumplings into the hot oil and deep-fry for 1–2 minutes until golden. Drain on paper towels.

Boil the noodles according to the package directions, cooking the pak choy in the same water for the final 30 seconds. Drain both.

Toss the noodles with the garlic oil and soy sauce, then divide among bowls. Top with the mushrooms, pak choy, tofu dumplings and spring onions (scallions). Serve with garlic broth and vinegar sambal.

Savoury Mushroom Rice in Cabbage Dome

Nasi Tim Jamur Sawi Putih

There's something comforting about a warm bowl of *nasi tim* – soft, savoury steamed rice flavoured with spiced shiitake mushroom. Simple yet comforting, it's especially popular in Chinese-Indonesian households. I first tried nasi tim as a child at a friend's home. Their version had chicken and mushrooms. In mine, I leave out the chicken, use more mushrooms and add layers of napa cabbage for extra veggies.

Traditionally, this is served in small portions. I've made a bigger version to share, with boiled eggs hidden inside to form a dome shape. Serve with light broth, spring onions (scallions), pickled cucumber and chillies.

Preparation time: 20 minutes, plus at least 3 hours marinating time
Cooking time: 1 hour

Serves 8

For the marinated eggs:

- 200 ml dark soy sauce
- 3 cloves garlic, minced
- 4 tablespoons honey
- 1 tablespoon sesame oil
- 3 bird's eye chillies, chopped finely
- 4 soft-boiled eggs, peeled

For the parcels:

- 3 tablespoons dark soy sauce
- 300 g/10½ oz (1½ cups) jasmine rice, well rinsed
- 40 g/1½ oz fresh root ginger, minced
- 1 napa cabbage, leaves separated
- 3 tablespoons sunflower oil
- 4 cloves garlic, minced
- 2 banana shallots, finely chopped
- 2 bird's eye chillies, finely chopped
- 400 g/14 oz shiitake or Portobello mushrooms, chopped into 1-cm/½-inch dice
- 2 teaspoons salt
- black pepper, to taste
- 3 tablespoons Sweet Soy Sauce (page 38)
- 3 tablespoons chopped parsley or celery leaves, to garnish
- Pickled Shallots, Cucumber and Chillies (page 53), to serve

To make the marinated eggs, combine all the ingredients except for the eggs in a deep container. Add 100 ml/3½ fl oz (scant ½ cup) of water and mix well. Add the eggs, ensuring they are submerged in the marinade. Cover and refrigerate for at least 3 hours or preferably overnight.

Meanwhile, in a saucepan, combine the rice, half of the ginger and ½ teaspoon of the salt. Pour in 300 ml/10 fl oz (1¼ cups) of water. Bring to the boil, then reduce the heat to medium-low and cook for 10–12 minutes, until the water has evaporated. Cover the pan, reduce the heat to very low and steam for another 10 minutes. (Alternatively, prepare the rice in a rice cooker.)

Meanwhile, remove the stalks from the cabbage leaves and set aside. Blanch the cabbage leaves only in a pan of boiling water. Set aside.

Heat the oil in a frying pan over medium heat. Add the garlic and shallots and sauté for 2–3 minutes. Add the remaining half of the ginger and the chillies and stir constantly for 1 minute. Add the mushrooms, season with the remaining 1½ teaspoons of salt and the pepper and sauté for 8 minutes until the mushrooms are caramelised. Add the sweet soy sauce and the cabbage stalks and simmer for 3–4 minutes, until softened. Taste: it should be balanced – not too sweet or salty. Check the seasoning and remove from the heat.

Lay two-thirds of the blanched cabbage leaves in a 20-cm/8-inch heatproof bowl. The cabbage should cover the bowl entirely. Add the mushroom mixture and half of the rice. Arrange the eggs in the bowl, spaced apart, adding some of the rice between them. Cover the surface with rice, then cover with the remaining cabbage leaves. Gently press the rice to make sure it is even. Steam in a larger steamer basket or wok, covered, for 30 minutes.

Using oven gloves (mitts), carefully transfer the bowl to a chopping (cutting) board lined with a dish towel. Put a large plate on top of the bowl, then quickly invert the bowl and lift it off. Sprinkle with parsley leaves and serve with pickles.

Grains and Legumes

Serealia dan biji-bijian

Across the Indonesian archipelago, food is more than sustenance – it is a living history, a reflection of culture and geography served on a plate. While rice (beras) is often seen as the nation's staple and celebrated in dishes from golden *nasi kuning* to the humble *nasi goreng*, it is far from the only source of nourishment.

I have vivid memories of walking through the terraced rice paddies of Tegalalang in Bali and witnessing *subak*, the traditional irrigation system. Equally striking was the sight of rice fields arranged in the shape of a giant spider web in Cancar, Manggarai, on the island of Flores, East Nusa Tenggara.

Indonesia's agricultural landscape is astonishingly diverse. Corn thrives in the drier regions of Eastern Indonesia, sorghum offers resilience and nutrition in tough soils and millet continues to be valued for its versatility. Legumes are just as vital: mung beans appear in both savoury stews and sweet treats while soybeans are transformed into beloved staples like tempeh, tofu, soy sauce and *tauco*, a rustic, fermented soy paste, similar to miso (see page 28). These plant-based ingredients carry rich culinary traditions while offering flavour, sustenance and variety.

Then there is sago, the starch harvested from the trunk of the sago palm, which remains the lifeblood of communities in Papua, Maluku and Sulawesi. Transformed into papeda, a silky porridge eaten with fragrant fish soups, or into pearls for desserts (see page 194), sago exemplifies the ingenious ways local crops have long shaped regional cuisines.

Together these grains and legumes tell a broader story of Indonesia's food heritage: one of resilience, adaptability and abundance. By celebrating them alongside rice we not only honour traditional food knowledge but also expand the possibilities of our own kitchens.

Crudités with Soybean-tahini Purèe

Lalapan, Kacang Kedelai Muda dengan Wijen Putih

White sesame, or *wijen putih*, is common in Indonesia, although we mostly use it in desserts. When I lived in Jakarta and couldn't find tahini or chickpeas (garbanzo beans), I made my own tahini from roasted white sesame and swapped chickpeas for young edamame. The result? A vibrant green, earthy and creamy purée that's perfect as a dip or spread. Edamame are mild, nutritious and widely available in Java. Paired with tahini, garlic, lime and olive oil, this purée is flavourful, balanced and ideal for sharing – a wholesome twist on a Middle Eastern classic with an Indonesian soul.

Preparation time: 15 minutes
Cooking time: 5 minutes

Serves 6–8

- 400 g/14 oz (2½ cups) fresh or frozen edamame
- 2–3 tablespoons tahini
- 2 cloves garlic, finely chopped
- 1 small onion, finely chopped
- 3 tablespoons extra-virgin olive oil, plus extra for drizzling
- 3–4 tablespoons lime juice
- 1 tablespoon cumin seeds, roasted and freshly ground
- 2–3 green bird's eye chillies (optional)
- salt, to taste

To serve:

- Pita bread
- Assorted raw vegetables, such as bell peppers, cucumbers and radishes

If using frozen edamame, bring a medium saucepan of salted water to the boil and boil the edamame for 5 minutes. Drain, then cool.

In a food processor or blender, combine the edamame, tahini, garlic, onion, olive oil, lime juice, cumin seeds and chillies, if using. Pour in 150 ml/5 fl oz (⅔ cup) of water and blend until smooth and creamy. Season with salt. Refrigerate until ready to serve.

Toast the pita in a dry frying pan or in the oven.

Spoon the green purée into a bowl, drizzle with olive oil and arrange the vegetables and pita around it. Serve immediately.

Bean and Cucumber Salad with Mint Yogurt

Selada Kacang-kacangan dengan Ketimu dan Yogurt daun Min

I grew up with peanuts, kidney beans and mung beans. It wasn't until adulthood that I realised just how diverse pulses (legumes) and beans are across the Indonesian archipelago. In Bogor, just outside Jakarta, you'll find earth pea (Bambara groundnut), native to the region. Indonesia is home to more than ten varieties of beans, including black-eyed peas and black soybeans. Fresh edamame – young soybeans in their pods – are also widely available in parts of Java and Bali.

This salad was inspired by that variety, and I've used whatever fresh beans I could find locally. I've added cumin, fennel, coriander and black pepper. While we often use the seeds of these spices, the leaves are just as fragrant and flavourful.

Preparation time: 25 minutes
Cooking time: 5 minutes

Serves 6–8

For the dressing:

- 100 ml/3½ fl oz (scant ½ cup) extra-virgin olive oil
- 2 red bird's eye chillies, finely chopped (optional)
- 1 clove garlic, minced
- juice of 1 large lime
- salt and black pepper, to taste

For the salad:

- 1 teaspoon cumin seeds
- 1 teaspoon fennel seeds
- 1 teaspoon coriander seeds
- 1 teaspoon black peppercorns
- 100 g/3½ oz (⅔ cup) broad (fava) beans
- 100 g/3½ oz (1 cup) edamame
- 50 g/1¾ oz (⅓ cup) peas
- 2 tablespoons honey
- 300 g/10½ oz (1½ cups) Greek yogurt
- 2 fresh corn cobs, kernels shaved
- ½ cucumber, halved lengthwise, seeded and cut into 1-cm/½-inch-thick half-moons (see Note)
- 200 g/7 oz cherry tomatoes, halved
- 100 g/3½ oz radishes, thinly sliced with a mandoline
- 2 banana shallots, thinly sliced
- 25 g/1 oz coriander (cilantro), coarsely chopped
- 25 g/1 oz parsley leaves, coarsely chopped
- bunch of mint leaves, to garnish

Combine all the dressing ingredients in a jar or sealable container, cover and shake to mix. Season to taste.

Make the salad. In a frying pan, combine the cumin seeds, fennel seeds, coriander seeds and black peppercorns. Roast over medium heat for 6–8 minutes, until fragrant. Set aside to cool, then grind with a mortar and pestle.

Bring a saucepan of water to the boil, add the broad (fava) beans and cook for 8 minutes. Drain and transfer them to a bowl of iced water to cool. Drain again and peel the outer skin from the beans. If you are OK with the bitterness from the skins, simply leave them on.

Boil the edamame and peas for 2–3 minutes. Drain, then transfer them to a bowl of iced water to stop the cooking process. Set aside to cool.

Combine the honey and yogurt in a bowl and set aside.

Combine all the remaining salad ingredients, including the beans, edamame and peas, but leaving out the mint, in a large bowl. Add the salad dressing and toss well.

Spread the yogurt mixture onto a large round serving plate. Sprinkle with one-quarter of the ground spices. Top with the salad, then sprinkle over the remaining spices and garnish with mint leaves. Serve immediately.

Note: Blend the discarded cucumber seeds with 500 ml/17 fl oz (generous 2 cups) of iced water and mint leaves for a refreshing drink.

Millet Salad with Tahini Sambal

Selada Jewawut dengan Sambal Wijen Putih

Long overlooked in Indonesian kitchens millet is making a quiet comeback. This humble ancient grain – often dismissed as bird food – is a nutritional powerhouse, packed with fibre, protein and essential minerals. Light, nutty and slightly chewy, it brings a fresh, modern texture to dishes where rice is typically expected.

Toasting the grains deepens their natural sweetness, making them the perfect base for bold, vibrant flavours. Here, millet takes centre stage, paired with a creamy tahini sambal – a riff on *cabuk rambak* from Solo, traditionally made with sesame and coconut. Used as a silky dressing, it pulls the dish together with richness and warmth.

Preparation time: 20 minutes
Cooking time: 20 minutes

Serves 4–6

- 150 g/5½ oz (generous 1 cup) millet
- salt, to taste
- 1 (400-g/14-oz) can butter (lima) beans, drained and rinsed
- black pepper, to taste
- 2 tablespoons lime juice
- 120 g/4¼ oz feta, crumbled
- 25 g/1 oz dill, coarsely chopped
- 25 g/1 oz basil leaves, coarsely chopped
- 1 quantity Tahini Sambal (page 36)
- 1 tablespoon honey
- 2 stalks celery, thinly sliced
- 100 g/3½ oz rainbow beetroots (beets), thinly sliced with a mandoline
- 5–6 radishes, thinly sliced with a mandoline
- 175 g/6 oz pomegranate seeds
- 50 g/1¾ oz (⅓ cup) roasted cashews, coarsely ground

In a medium saucepan, toast the millet over medium heat without oil for 4–5 minutes, until light golden brown. Set aside for 3–4 minutes to cool a little.

Add 400 ml/14 fl oz (1⅔ cups) of water and a pinch of salt to the pan and mix well. Bring to the boil, then reduce the heat and simmer for 15 minutes, until the millet is cooked through. Set aside to cool slightly, then fluff with a fork and transfer to a large serving plate to cool to room temperature.

To assemble the salad, combine the cooked millet and butter (lima) beans. Season with salt, pepper and lime juice. Add half of the crumbled feta and a quarter of the chopped herbs. Stir in half of the tahini sambal and the honey and gently toss.

Arrange the salad on a serving plate. Add the remaining tahini sambal, remaining feta and herbs. Sprinkle with pomegranate seeds and cashews and serve.

Warm Sorghum Salad with Smoked Tomato Sambal

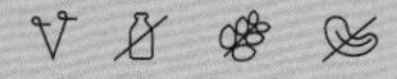

Selada Sorgum Hangat dengan Tomat Sambal Asap

A harmony of flavours and textures, this dish combines the nutty chew of sorghum, the sweet tang of pineapple pickles, the delicate creaminess of griddled (grilled) tofu and the bold, smoky heat of tomato sambal.

Sorghum – an ancient, nutrient-rich grain with subtle earthiness – forms a hearty base, soaking up the vibrant flavours of the island of Flores. The pineapple pickles cut through with bright acidity, balancing the richness. Tofu brings a soft, mellow contrast, while the sambal ties it all together with umami, smoke and spice. I hope Mama Maria (see page 166) approves of my take on sorghum.

Preparation time: 20 minutes, plus overnight soaking time
Cooking time: 35 minutes

Serves 4

* 140 g/5 oz (2/3 cup) sorghum, soaked overnight, or quinoa
* 1 teaspoon salt, plus extra to taste
* 1 (400-g/14-oz) block Beetroot Tofu (page 59), cut into 4 slabs
* black pepper, to taste
* Pickled Pineapple (page 48)
* 4 baby gem lettuces, halved
* sunflower oil, for drizzling
* 1 quantity Smoked Tomato Sambal (page 36)

Drain the sorghum and place in a medium saucepan along with 750 ml/25 fl oz (3 cups) of water and 1 teaspoon of salt. Bring to the boil, then reduce to a simmer, cover and cook for 20 minutes.

Add the tofu to the pan, then season with salt and pepper. Cover and cook for another 10 minutes. Remove from the heat and set aside for 5 minutes.

To serve, place the sorghum mixture on a large serving platter and top with the tofu and charred lettuces. Garnish with basil and serve with a side of the smoked tomato sambal.

Vegetable Coconut Curry with Rice Cakes

Ketupat Sayur

Ketupat is a traditional Indonesian rice cake, wrapped in woven coconut leaves and boiled until firm. Commonly served during Lebaran (Eid al-Fitr), it has a compact, slightly chewy texture and is often paired with rich, flavourful dishes. It also carries symbolic meaning – gratitude and togetherness. A simpler version, *lontong*, is made by boiling rice in banana leaves, making it more practical for everyday meals.

One of my most memorable servings was at Bumi Serpong Market near Jakarta, where I was photographed eating *lontong sayur* – a moment that later became the cover of my book *Jakarta Bites*.

Preparation time: 20 minutes
Cooking time: 15 minutes

Serves 4–6

- 1 quantity Compressed Rice (page 42), cut into bite-size pieces
- 1 quantity Yellow Spice Paste (page 32)
- 2 stalks lemongrass, crushed and tied into a knot
- 3 makrut lime leaves
- 400 ml/14 fl oz (1⅔ cups) coconut milk
- 1 large chayote, peeled and cut into matchsticks
- 100 g/3½ oz long beans or French beans, cut into 3-cm/1¼-inch pieces
- 1½ carrots, cut into 5-mm/¼-inch discs
- 200 g/7 oz Fresh Tofu (page 44) or Smoked Tofu (page 44)
- 1 tablespoon miso paste
- 1 tablespoon coconut sugar
- salt and black pepper, to taste
- 2–3 eggs
- 3 tablespoons Crispy Shallots (page 41), to serve

If you have prepared the compressed rice in advance, remove from the refrigerator 1 hour before, so it is not too cold.

Combine the paste, lemongrass and makrut lime leaves in a medium pan. Pour in 200 ml/7 fl oz (scant 1 cup) of water and 200 ml/7 fl oz (scant 1 cup) of coconut milk. Bring to the boil, then add the chayote, beans, carrots and tofu and simmer for 10–12 minutes, until all the vegetables are soft. Add the miso and coconut sugar. Mix well. Season with salt and pepper.

Meanwhile, put the eggs into a small saucepan of water. Bring to the boil and boil for 6–7 minutes. Drain, then transfer to a bowl of cold water to stop the cooking process. When cool enough to handle, peel the eggs and slice.

Add the remaining coconut milk to the vegetable mixture. Bring to the boil, then simmer for 2–3 minutes. Season with salt.

To serve, divide the rice cakes among 4 bowls and ladle over the vegetable mixture. Add 1–2 sliced eggs to each bowl and top with crispy shallots.

Pearl Barley, Pea and Tempeh Coconut Curry

Jali-Jali, Peas dan Tempe Kari

Pearl barley *(jali-jali)* is a nutritious, versatile grain traditionally used in sweet porridges, especially on Sumatra. One of my favourite preparations of it is in a hearty one-pot curry with tempeh. Barley's chewy texture and mild, nutty flavour soak up Indonesian spices beautifully. It offers a wholesome base, while tempeh – the country's iconic fermented soybean cake – brings bite and rich umami.

Simmered in a coconut-based broth with chillies, lemongrass and makrut lime leaves, the dish is both comforting and full of authentic flavour. This curry bridges tradition and innovation, proving Indonesian ingredients can shine in new ways.

Preparation time: 10 minutes
Cooking time: 35–45 minutes

Serves 4–6

- 2 tablespoons coconut oil
- 1–2 large banana shallots, thinly sliced
- 4 cloves garlic, finely chopped
- 2–3 red bird's eye chillies, finely chopped
- 2 large red chillies, finely chopped
- 1 stalk lemongrass, crushed and tied into a knot
- 4 makrut lime leaves
- 1 teaspoon ground coriander
- 1 teaspoon ground turmeric
- 200 g/7 oz (1 cup) pearl barley
- salt and black pepper, to taste
- 200 g/7 oz tempeh, cut into 1-cm/½-inch chunks
- 400 ml/14 fl oz (1⅔ cups) coconut milk
- 100 g/3½ oz (⅔ cup) frozen peas
- 100 g/3½ oz spinach leaves

Heat the coconut oil in a medium saucepan over medium heat. Add the shallots and garlic and cook for 3 minutes, then add the chillies, lemongrass, makrut lime leaves, coriander and turmeric. Quickly rinse the pearl barley, then add it to the pan. Pour in 750 ml/25 fl oz (3 cups) of water and bring to the boil. Season with salt and pepper, then add the tempeh and simmer for 30–35 minutes, until the water has evaporated and the pearl barley is tender.

Add the coconut milk and mix well, then add the frozen peas, bring to the boil and cook for 2–3 minutes. Add the spinach and cook for a final minute. Season with salt.

Discard the lemongrass and makrut lime leaves and serve.

Corn and Red Bean Stew
Jagung Bose

Flores, in East Nusa Tenggara, left a deep impression on me, with its stunning landscapes and the cultural richness of the Sikka tribe. During my visit, the women welcomed me with warmth – dressing me in traditional clothes and inviting me to dance, sing and try their handmade cigarettes.

This traditional corn stew, often made with red beans, is a regional staple that's becoming rare as rice gains popularity – It's hearty, creamy and full of flavour. In my version, I use fresh corn, basil and crispy tempeh for texture.

Preparation time: 10 minutes
Cooking time: 50 minutes

Serves 6

* 4 fresh corn cobs
* 6 cloves garlic: 4 whole and 2 chopped
* 2 tablespoons sunflower oil
* 2 banana shallots, chopped
* 2–3 bird's eye chillies
* 1 (400-g/14-oz) can kidney beans in water, drained and rinsed
* 400 ml/14 fl oz (1⅔ cups) coconut milk
* small bunch of basil
* salt and black pepper, to taste
* small bunch of watercress, to serve
* Deep-fried Tempeh (page 76), cubed, for topping (optional)

Cut the kernels from the cobs of sweetcorn. Set the kernels aside and place the cobs in a saucepan (halve if they don't fit). Add the whole garlic cloves and 1 litre/35 fl oz (4 cups) of water and boil for 30 minutes. Set aside.

Heat the oil in a frying pan over medium heat. Add the shallots and chopped garlic and sauté for 2 minutes. Add the chillies and cook for another minute. Stir in the kidney beans and add 200 ml/7 fl oz (scant 1 cup) of the corn stock. Bring to the boil and simmer for 10 minutes.

Add the coconut milk and basil and bring back to the boil, then season with salt and pepper. Gradually add the corn kernels but do not mix. This helps to warm them through while preserving the vibrant colour. Cover and simmer for 5 minutes, until steaming hot.

To serve, pour 3 ladles of the stew into individual bowls, making sure you have some corn and red beans in each bowl. Place a small bunch of watercress in the middle of each and fried tempeh on top. Serve.

Sorghum and Tempeh Cakes with Sambal

Sorgum Perkedel Tempe dan Dabu-dabu

The first time I prepared sorghum was over ten years ago for a charity dinner in Jakarta. Each time I make it, I think of Mama Maria Loretha – a strong, inspiring community leader and my food hero. We met when we both received community service awards: I was recognised for my work with Cheshire Home, supporting people with disabilities, and Mama Maria was honoured for her work promoting sorghum and food diversity in Nusa Tenggara.

Sorghum, from the island of Flores, is an ancient, gluten-free grain, traditionally used in porridges, mixed with rice or made into fermented drinks. It has a nutty taste and a hearty texture.

I love how tempeh, sambal and sorghum together reflect the richness of Indonesian food – combining traditional ingredients with a modern touch.

Preparation time: 30–35 minutes, plus overnight soaking time
Cooking time: 35–40 minutes

Serves 4

- 200 g/7 oz (1 cup) sorghum, soaked overnight, or quinoa
- 7–10 baby beetroots (beets), well rinsed and unpeeled (500 g/1 lb 2 oz)
- juice of 1 lime
- 2 avocados
- salt, to taste
- small handful of basil, plus extra to garnish
- 1 quantity Chilli and Tomato Sambal (page 36)
- 80 g/2¾ oz (5½ cups) mixed salad leaves

For the tempeh cakes:

- 1 (200-g/7-oz) block tempeh
- 200 g/7 oz (1⅓ cups) frozen peas
- ½ teaspoon chilli powder
- ½ teaspoon white pepper
- 2 eggs
- 2 tablespoons cornflour (cornstarch)
- 4 tablespoons sliced spring onions (scallions)
- salt, to taste
- sunflower oil, for deep-frying

Drain and rinse the sorghum. In a large saucepan, combine the sorghum, beetroots (beets) and 750 ml/25 fl oz (3 cups) of water. Bring to the boil, then reduce the heat to medium and cook until the water has evaporated and both the sorghum and beetroots are softened. Transfer to a large plate and set aside to cool.

Meanwhile, make the tempeh cakes. Combine the tempeh, peas, chilli powder and pepper in a food processor and blend coarsely, then transfer to a medium bowl. Add the eggs, cornflour (cornstarch) and spring onions (scallions) and season with salt. Mix well. Take heaped tablespoons of the mixture and shape into patties. Repeat until all the mixture is used up.

Heat enough sunflower oil for deep-frying in a large frying pan over medium heat. The oil is ready when a cube of bread dropped in sizzles on contact and turns golden in 10–15 seconds. (Alternatively, use a thermometer and heat to 180°C/350°F.)

Fry 2–3 tempeh cakes at a time for 2 minutes, until golden brown on both sides. Remove with a slotted spoon to drain on a plate lined with paper towels. Repeat until all the cakes are cooked. Keep warm in a low-temperature oven, if needed.

Cut the beetroots into quarters and place in a bowl. Add the lime juice. Cut the avocados into 1-cm/½-inch cubes and add to the bowl. Season with salt and mix well, then add the basil and mix again.

In a separate bowl, add the sambal to the sorghum and toss to combine. Season with salt. Add the mixed salad leaves and toss again.

Serve the sorghum and beetroot salads topped with the tempeh cakes, garnished with extra basil.

Corn and Spinach Risotto with Corn Fritters

Barrobo dengan Perkedel Jagung

This dish was inspired by *barrobo*, a corn-based dish from Central Sulawesi, similar to *tinutuan* – the comforting rice and corn porridge from Manado, North Sulawesi. (I wrote about tinutuan in *The Indonesian Table*.) Both dishes evoke the warmth of nostalgic childhood meals. I like to reimagine beloved regional dishes in a more modern way.

I turned it into a corn risotto, infused with lemongrass and topped with *kemangi sambal* – it's a dish that bridges past and present.

Here, the sweetcorn is paired with leafy greens, and instead of the usual potato cake, I've added corn fritters for crunch. The creamy base and earthy flavours make it grounding and familiar.

Preparation time: 25 minutes
Cooking time: 35 minutes

Serves 4

For the corn fritters:

- 250 g/9 oz (1½ cups) fresh or canned sweetcorn
- 3 makrut lime leaves, centre stem removed and thinly sliced
- 2 cloves garlic, grated
- 2 spring onions (scallions), finely chopped
- 1–2 red bird's eye chillies, finely chopped
- 1 banana shallot, finely chopped
- 6 tablespoons rice flour
- 4 tablespoons cornflour (cornstarch)
- ½ teaspoon salt
- ½ teaspoon white pepper
- 500 ml/17 fl oz (generous 2 cups) sunflower oil, for deep-frying

For the risotto:

- 2 tablespoons coconut oil or sunflower oil
- 2 banana shallots, finely chopped
- 2 cloves garlic, finely chopped
- 200 g/7 oz (generous 1 cup) risotto rice
- 2 stalks lemongrass, crushed and tied into a knot
- ½ teaspoon salt, plus extra to season
- 3 fresh corn cobs, kernels removed
- 225 g/8 oz (3 cups) spinach
- black pepper, to taste
- large handful of basil leaves, to garnish
- Shallot Sambal (page 36), to serve (optional)

First, make the corn fritters. If using canned sweetcorn, drain well. Transfer the sweetcorn to a food processor and pulse for 10 seconds, until you have a coarse purée.

In a large bowl, combine the puréed sweetcorn, makrut lime leaves, garlic, spring onions (scallions), chillies and shallot and mix well. Stir in the rice flour and cornflour (cornstarch) until the mixture is thick but still easy to mix. Season with salt and white pepper. If needed, add 2–3 tablespoons of cold water to thin out the mixture slightly.

Heat the sunflower oil in a wok or deep saucepan over medium heat. The oil is ready when a cube of bread dropped in sizzles on contact and turns golden in 10–15 seconds. (Alternatively, use a thermometer and heat to 180°C/350°F.)

Scoop tablespoons of the sweetcorn mixture and flatten each slightly into a patty. Carefully lower 5–6 patties into the oil and deep-fry for 2–3 minutes on each side until golden brown. Using a slotted spoon, transfer the fritters to a plate lined with paper towels to drain. Transfer to a baking sheet and keep the fritters warm in a low oven (80°C/175°F). Repeat with the remaining fritters.

Heat the oil for the risotto in a medium saucepan over medium heat. Add the shallots and garlic and sauté for 7 minutes, until softened and fragrant. Add the rice, lemongrass and ½ teaspoon of the salt. Add 200 ml/7 fl oz (scant 1 cup) of hot water and bring to the boil. Reduce the heat to medium-low, cover and simmer for 2–3 minutes. Continue adding the remaining 600 ml/20 fl oz (2½ cups) of hot water, 1–2 ladlefuls at a time, allowing each addition to be absorbed before adding more, and cook until the rice is al dente, about 14 minutes.

Add the corn kernels and cook for 2 minutes. Season with pepper. Add the spinach and mix well. Add up to 100 ml/3½ fl oz (scant ½ cup) of hot water until you have your desired consistency. Shake the pan to check if the rice can easily move. If not, add a touch more water. Season with salt and pepper.

Serve the risotto on individual plates, topped with the corn fritters. Garnish with basil and serve with shallot sambal on the side.

Tropical Fruits

Buah-buahan Tropis

Some of my fondest childhood memories involve tropical fruit – like sitting high up in a tree, eating mangoes picked fresh from the branch. The flavours still linger in my mind: the sweet juiciness of *mangga kuini* with its deep orange flesh, the creamy richness of different banana varieties and the bright, tangy notes of mangoesteen. Each bite was a perfect harmony of taste and texture.

In Manado, North Sulawesi, where I grew up, the air was filled with the fragrance of water apple, pineapple and guava. Coconut and soursop brought cool relief on hot days, their hydrating freshness always a welcome treat. Later, when I lived in South Jakarta, my garden was home to papaya, jackfruit and pomelo trees. There's nothing quite like eating ripe, sun-warmed fruit you've grown yourself.

Over the years, the landscape of fruit in Indonesia has evolved. Fruits that weren't part of my childhood – like watermelon, various other melons and dragon fruit – are now commonplace in markets across the country. During a recent trip to Jakarta, I was stunned to see a tray of six strawberries, grown locally by a Japanese company, selling for £8 (US$10). It's a sign of how Indonesia's fertile soil and favourable climate, combined with modern farming techniques, have sparked global interest in fruit cultivation here.

Tropical fruits are incredibly versatile. While many shine best when eaten fresh, they're also used in both sweet and savoury dishes. Ripe fruit is delicious in smoothies, juices, salads and desserts, while unripe fruit adds a tangy twist to dishes like Rendang (page 180) and Pineapple, Tofu and Tempeh Curry (page 178).

Tropical Fruit with Kefir

Buah Tropis dengan Yogurt Kefir

When travelling through Indonesia – especially outside the cities – you'll often spot small roadside fruit stalls. The more remote the area, the more local the selection: papaya, pineapple and small bananas are all common sights. Ripe fruit isn't typically seen as breakfast, but more as an anytime snack or a sweet finish to a meal. This simple 'recipe' celebrates tropical fruits in their natural form. No elaborate plating, just scoop and enjoy.

If you're serving papaya on its own, a squeeze of lime brightens the flavour, especially with milder or overly sweet varieties. Pineapple benefits from the same trick of balance – a light sprinkle of salt brings out its natural sweetness. The kefir here is a gentle nod to *dadih*, the traditional buffalo milk yogurt of West Sumatra.

Preparation time: 30 minutes

Serves 8

* 2 ripe mangoes
* 2 dragon fruits
* 1 small ripe papaya
* 1 lime, halved
* 4–6 passion fruits
* 400 g/14 oz (2 cups) kefir or Greek yogurt
* handful of roasted cashews, sunflower seeds or any seeds of choice, to garnish (optional)
* handful of mint leaves, to garnish (optional)

Cut the mango, dragon fruit and papaya into cubes. Squeeze lime juice over the papaya. Place the mixed fruit into a large serving bowl or individual bowls and top with passion fruit and kefir and sprinkle with the seeds. Serve.

Variation:

- **Papaya Boat**

  Cut a papaya in half lengthwise. Using a measuring spoon, scoop out the flesh into small spheres. Squeeze the lime juice over the papaya. Scoop out balls of the mango and dragon fruit. Combine the fruit in the papaya shell. Top with passion fruit pulp for brightness.

Mango Salad with Dabu-dabu Strawberries

Selada Mangga dan Dabu-Dabu Stroberi

Strawberries are my favourite summer fruit – and British ones are truly the best. Living in the countryside, I'm lucky to pick them fresh from local farms during the season. Inspired by the bold flavours of Manado's *dabu-dabu*, this version uses strawberries for a bright, unexpected twist. Their natural sweetness and tartness balance the heat of chillies, the sharpness of shallots and the zing of lime juice. The result is a fiery, fruit-forward relish that still captures the essence of the original.

Paired with juicy mango, it becomes even more dynamic. The tropical sweetness complements the tangy-spicy mix, which is perfect with roasted vegetables or a fresh salad. There's no oil – just a splash of water to round out the acidity.

Preparation time: 15 minutes

Serves 4

* 2 ripe mangoes, peeled and cut into bite-size pieces
* 250 g/9 oz mixed salad leaves
* bunch of basil

For the dabu-dabu strawberries:

* 200 g/7 oz strawberries, washed and quartered
* 1 banana shallot, finely chopped
* 2–3 red bird's eye chillies, finely chopped
* juice of 2 limes
* salt, to taste

To make the dabu-dabu strawberries, combine all the ingredients with 3 tablespoons of water in a large bowl. Mix well and season with salt.

Add the mangoes to the bowl and gently mix until evenly coated. Add the salad leaves and toss until well combined.

Transfer the mixture to a large serving plate. Garnish with the basil leaves and serve immediately.

Papaya Salad with Chillies, Ginger, Mint and Roasted Cashews

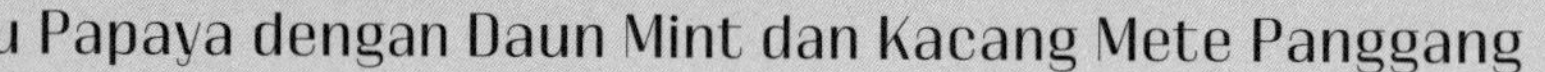

Gohu Papaya dengan Daun Mint dan Kacang Mete Panggang

This dish brings back fond memories of my childhood in Manado, North Sulawesi. It's a vibrant and refreshing salad made with crisp, unripe papaya, fresh chillies for fiery heat, warm ginger, tangy vinegar and fragrant mint leaves – a perfect balance of flavours.

Mint was a common ingredient in my grandmother's time but is rarely used today. Its cooling aroma adds a nostalgic touch to the dish. The crunch of the papaya, soaked in the bold, zesty dressing, makes every bite both invigorating and addictive. I add roasted cashews for extra texture and richness. With its spicy, sour and slightly sweet notes, this delicious salad is a true taste of home.

Preparation time: 10 minutes, plus 30 minutes chilling time

Serves 6

* 1 small unripe papaya
* small bunch of mint leaves, to garnish
* 40 g/1½ oz (scant ⅓ cup) roasted cashews, coarsely ground, to garnish

For the dressing:

* 2 large red chillies, thinly sliced
* 1 red bird's eye chilli, finely chopped (optional)
* 10 g/¼ oz fresh root ginger, grated
* 1 teaspoon salt
* 3½ tablespoons Simple Syrup (page 38)
* 3½ tablespoons rice vinegar, apple cider vinegar or white wine vinegar

First, make the dressing. Combine all the ingredients in a bowl and stir in 100 ml/3½ fl oz (scant ½ cup) of cold water.

Using a vegetable peeler, shave the papaya into ribbons. Combine the papaya and dressing in a large serving bowl and refrigerate for at least 30 minutes.

When ready to serve, garnish with the mint leaves and cashews.

Coconut and Roasted Vegetable Curry
Kelapa dan Sayur Panggang Kari

Inspired by traditional chicken *tuturuga* from Manado, this plant-based version captures all the rich, comforting flavours of the original. Fragrant with coconut milk, spices and herbs, it's satisfying and full of depth. You can swap the roasted vegetables for jackfruit or stir in chayote, long beans, cauliflower or cabbage – whatever's in season or already in your kitchen.

For serving, it's just as flexible: pair it with rice, or try something unexpected like pasta, sorghum or quinoa for a fun twist. However you plate it, this is a celebration of flavour, comfort and the joy of cooking with what you have.

Preparation time: 25 minutes
Cooking time: 40–45 minutes

Serves 4–6

For the curry:

* 2 courgettes (zucchini), cut into 4-cm/1½-inch chunks
* 1 aubergine (eggplant), cut into 4-cm/1½-inch chunks
* 500 g/1 lb 2 oz pumpkin or butternut squash, cut into 4-cm/1½-inch chunks
* 2 teaspoons salt
* 2 teaspoons black pepper
* 2 tablespoons coconut oil or sunflower oil
* 1 quantity Yellow Spice Paste (page 32)
* 1 stalk lemongrass, crushed and tied into a knot
* 3 makrut lime leaves, roughly torn
* 400 ml/14 fl oz (1⅔ cups) coconut milk
* 200 g/7 oz Smoked Tofu (page 44), cut into bite-size pieces
* 225 g/8 oz spinach
* 2 tablespoons chopped basil
* steamed rice or pasta, to serve

Preheat the oven to 200°C/400°F/Gas Mark 6.

Arrange the courgettes (zucchini), aubergine (eggplant) and pumpkin on separate baking sheets and season with a teaspoon each of the salt and pepper. Roast the courgettes and aubergine for 15–20 minutes, until tender and slightly caramelised. Remove from the oven.

Roast the pumpkin for another 15 minutes, until tender. Remove from the oven and set aside.

Meanwhile, heat the oil in a wok or frying pan over medium-high heat. Add the spice paste and sauté for 5–6 minutes, until fragrant. Add the lemongrass and makrut lime leaves, then pour in the coconut milk and 400 ml/14 fl oz (1⅔ cups) of water and bring to the boil. Add the tofu, reduce the heat to medium-low and simmer for 10 minutes. Season with the remaining teaspoon each of salt and pepper.

Stir in all the roasted vegetables and mix well, then bring to the boil and cook for another 6 minutes. Add the spinach and basil and cook for 2 minutes. Check the seasoning.

Serve hot with steamed rice.

Fruit and Cucumber Salad with Tamarind-chilli Sauce
Rujak Buah dan Mentimun

Rujak is a beloved Indonesian fruit salad with countless regional variations, each balancing sweet, sour, spicy and savoury flavours. Preparation styles differ too – some regions grind fried peanuts into the sauce for extra depth.

This simple yet refreshing version combines crisp unripe mango, cucumber, jicama and juicy pomelo. I've swapped pomelo and water apple for grapefruit and eating apple – easy substitutes that keep the brightness and crunch.

Preparation time: 30 minutes

Serves 12

* 2 apples, cut into wedges
* 2 tablespoons lime juice
* 1 unripe mango, peeled and thinly sliced
* 1 small pineapple, peeled, eyes removed and cut into small wedges
* 200 g/7 oz pomelo flesh or 1 grapefruit, segmented
* 1 cucumber, peeled into ribbons
* 1 jicama (optional)
* roasted cashews, coarsely ground, for sprinkling (optional)

For the sauce:

* 2–3 red bird's eye chillies, finely chopped
* 80 ml/2¾ fl oz (⅓ cup) coconut sugar
* 100 ml/3½ fl oz (scant ½ cup) Tamarind Paste (page 32)
* pinch of salt

In a large bowl, combine the apple wedges, lime juice and 300 ml/10 fl oz (1¼ cups) of cold water to prevent the apples from turning brown.

Make the sauce. Using a pestle and mortar, grind the chillies to a paste with the coconut sugar.

Transfer the mixture to a bowl and stir in the tamarind paste. Season with salt.

Drain the apples. Place all the fruits in a large platter, drizzle with the sauce, sprinkle with the roasted cashews and serve.

Coconut Risotto with Potato Sambal

Nasi Kuning Dengan Sambal Kentang

I've always loved *nasi kuning* – fragrant turmeric and coconut rice that's found across the Indonesian archipelago. In this version, the rich, aromatic rice is paired with sweet-and-spicy shiitake mushrooms and a side of potato sambal for extra texture and depth.

The inspiration comes from my hometown of Manado, where nasi kuning is traditionally served with shredded spicy tuna, tomato sambal and potato sambal, all neatly wrapped in yellow palm leaves. While this plate may take a different form, the flavours remain comfortingly familiar.

The potato sambal can be made in advance – it keeps well in a jar for up to a week.

Preparation time: 25 minutes
Cooking time: 50 minutes

Serves 4–6

For the potato sambal:
- coconut oil, for deep-frying
- 2 waxy potatoes, cut into thin matchsticks
- salt, to taste
- 2 banana shallots, thinly sliced
- 3 cloves garlic, sliced
- 2 bird's eye chillies, finely chopped
- 2 large chillies, finely chopped

For the risotto:
- 15 g/½ oz fresh turmeric or 1 teaspoon ground turmeric
- 400 ml/14 fl oz (1⅔ cups) coconut milk
- salt, to taste
- 2 tablespoons coconut oil or sunflower oil
- 2 shallots, finely chopped
- 400 g/14 oz (generous 2 cups) Arborio or carnaroli rice
- 2 stalks lemongrass, crushed and tied into a knot
- 4 dried or fresh makrut lime leaves
- 1 long pandan leaf, sliced into thirds (optional)

For the mushrooms:
- 3 tablespoons coconut oil or sunflower oil
- 2 shallots, finely chopped
- 3 cloves garlic, finely chopped
- 600 g/1 lb 5 oz shiitake mushrooms, sliced
- 1 red bird's eye chillies, finely chopped
- 3 tablespoons Sweet Soy Sauce (page 38)
- 2 tablespoon light soy sauce
- salt and black pepper, to taste

First, make the potato sambal. Heat the oil for deep-frying in a wok or deep saucepan over medium heat. The oil is ready when a cube of bread dropped in sizzles on contact and turns golden in 10–15 seconds. (Alternatively, use a thermometer and heat to 180°C/350°F.)

Season the potatoes with salt and deep-fry for 2–3 minutes on each side, until golden. Using a slotted spoon, transfer the potatoes to a plate lined with paper towels.

Remove all but 3 tablespoons of oil from the pan. Add the shallots, garlic and chillies and sauté over medium heat for 4 minutes, until caramelised. Season with salt.

Add the potatoes and mix well. Transfer to a plate and set aside to cool.

Next, make the risotto. If using fresh turmeric, blend the turmeric with 100 ml/3½ fl oz (scant ½ cup) of water, then strain into a medium saucepan. If using ground turmeric, simply add it to the water and mix well. Add the coconut milk and 1.4 L / 47 fl oz (generous 5¾ cups) of hot water to the pan and bring to the boil, then keep hot on a low simmer. Season with salt.

Heat the oil in a sauté pan over medium-high heat. Add the shallots and sauté until softened, then add the rice and stir for 2–3 minutes, until the grains are fully coated. Add the lemongrass, makrut lime leaves and pandan leaf, if using, and a ladleful of the hot turmeric-coconut stock. Stir until most of the liquid has been absorbed. Add another ladle of stock and repeat for 10–12 minutes, until the rice is nearly al dente.

Meanwhile, prepare the mushrooms. Heat the oil in a frying pan over medium-high heat. Add the shallots and garlic and sauté for 2–3 minutes, until the shallots are softened. Add the mushrooms, chillies, both soy sauces and a pinch of salt and sauté for 10 minutes over medium heat.

Pour in 100 ml/3½ fl oz (scant ½ cup) of water and simmer for 10 minutes. Season with pepper. Cook for another 10 minutes until the mushrooms are softened and the water has evaporated.

Taste the risotto. If necessary, add a touch of salt. Remove the lemongrass, lime and pandan leaf. Serve on individual plates, topped with the mushrooms and 2 tablespoons of potato sambal.

Variation:

For a simpler take, replace the mushrooms and potato sambal with 200 g/7 oz of asparagus. Boil for 3–4 minutes, until just tender. Drain well, then toss with 1 teaspoon of coconut oil. Serve the spears on top of each portion of the risotto.

Pineapple, Tofu and Tempeh Curry

Kalio Nanas, Tahu dan Tempe

Kalio is a rich Indonesian curry from West Sumatra, considered a precursor to *rendang*. Unlike rendang, which is dry and deeply caramelised, kalio is cooked for less time, resulting in a thick, aromatic sauce that coats the ingredients. Flavoured with coconut milk, galangal, lemongrass, turmeric and chilli, kalio is bold yet balanced. Although it is traditionally made with beef or chicken, it's easily adapted to plant-based options. This standout variation pairs savoury tempeh with the bright sweetness of pineapple – a vibrant twist on a classic dish.

Preparation time: 20 minutes
Cooking time: 15–20 minutes

Serves 4–6

- 4 tablespoons coconut oil or sunflower oil
- 1 quantity Yellow Spice Paste (page 32)
- 1 small pineapple, peeled, cored and cut into 2-cm/¾-inch cubes
- 200 g/7 oz Fresh Tofu (page 44) or Smoked Tofu (page 44)
- 200 g/7 oz tempeh
- 4 makrut lime leaves, torn
- 1 stalk lemongrass, crushed and tied in a knot
- 400 ml/14 fl oz (1⅔ cups) coconut milk
- ½ teaspoon salt
- black pepper, to taste
- juice of 1 lime
- 1 large red chilli, thinly sliced, to garnish
- steamed rice, to serve

Heat 2 tablespoons of the oil in a saucepan over medium heat. Add the spice paste and cook for 5 minutes. Add the pineapple, tofu, tempeh, makrut lime leaves and lemongrass, gently mix and cook for 2 minutes. Pour in half of the coconut milk and 800 ml/27 fl oz (3½ cups) of water. Bring to the boil, then reduce the heat to medium-low. Cover and simmer for 10 minutes, until the pineapple is softened.

Add the remaining coconut milk and season with the salt, pepper and lime juice. Discard the lemongrass and makrut lime leaves.

Garnish with the chilli and serve with rice.

Jackfruit Rendang

Rendang Nangka Muda

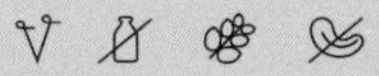

Rendang nangka, or unripe jackfruit rendang, is a cherished West Sumatran dish, often served alongside its beef counterpart. Slow-cooked in coconut milk and spices, the jackfruit becomes tender and deeply infused with rich, aromatic flavours. As the sauce reduces, it thickens into a savoury-sweet glaze that clings to each piece.

Popular among vegetarians, this dish stays true to the essence of traditional rendang. Roasted coconut paste adds depth and colour, while using young jackfruit offers a more sustainable alternative. Whether made with local leaves, tempeh or tofu, rendang nangka reflects Indonesia's enduring philosophy of cooking with patience, purpose and respect for nature.

Preparation time: 20 minutes
Cooking time: 1¾ hours

Serves 6–8

For the curry:

- 50 g/1¾ oz (⅔ cup) unsweetened desiccated coconut
- 2–3 tablespoons coconut oil or sunflower oil
- 3 (565-g/20-oz) cans young green jackfruit in water or brine, drained
- 1.2 litres/40 fl oz (5 cups) coconut milk
- 2 tablespoons tamarind paste
- 7 makrut lime leaves, torn
- 2 star anise
- 2 stalks lemongrass, crushed and tied in a knot
- 1 (3-cm/1¼-inch) cinnamon stick
- 1 turmeric leaf (optional)
- 1 teaspoon salt, or to taste
- 1 teaspoon black pepper, or to taste
- steamed rice, to serve
- Pickled Pineapple (page 78), to serve

For the chilli paste:

- 4 cloves garlic, sliced
- 2 small banana shallots, sliced
- 20 g/¾ oz fresh root ginger, sliced
- 10 g/¼ oz galangal, thinly sliced
- 4 red bird's eye chillies, coarsely chopped
- 2 large red chillies, coarsely chopped

Heat a frying pan over medium heat. Add the desiccated coconut and dry-roast until it is dark in colour but not burned.

Transfer to a spice grinder or pestle and mortar and grind until it transforms from a fine powder into an oily paste. Set aside.

Meanwhile, make the chilli paste. Combine all the ingredients in a small blender and blend into a smooth paste.

Heat the oil in a frying pan over medium heat, add the chilli paste and sauté for 3–4 minutes. Add the jackfruit and coconut milk, then stir in the remaining curry ingredients. Bring to the boil, then simmer for 1 hour, stirring occasionally to prevent the mixture from sticking, until the liquid has reduced by half.

Add the coconut paste to the jackfruit mixture and mix well. Reduce the heat to medium-low and simmer for another 30 minutes, until the liquid has reduced further.

Increase the heat to high and cook for a final 12 minutes, stirring constantly, until all the liquid has evaporated and the rendang is dark brown and caramelised. Season to taste.

Serve with steamed rice and pickled pineapple.

Desserts and Drinks

Kue dan Minuman

In Indonesia, desserts and drinks are part of daily rhythm. They refresh on hot afternoons, comfort at the close of a meal and bring colour to family gatherings. Their forms are wide-ranging – silky puddings, fragrant cakes, icy sweets and restorative tonics.

Chocolate and palm sugar may be the most familiar flavours – from the nostalgic Chocolate Pudding with Vanilla Custard (page 192) to the deep notes of Black Glutinous Rice Pudding with Mango (page 197). Yet the chapter goes far beyond. Coconut takes centre stage in Klappertaart with Strawberries (page 196) and Manado-style Coconut Macarons (pages 202). Sago pearls gleam in Blue Sago Pudding with Mango (pages 194). Fruits brighten Banana and Pineapple Cake (page 200) and the tart-sweet Lime Loaf with Sweet Kolak Sauce (pages 199).

The drinks are just as inventive: tangy Sour Turmeric (page 184), spiced and soothing Bajigur (pages 184), playful Es Cendol with pandan jelly (page 188) and Sekoteng, a ginger broth brimming with nuts, mung beans and tapioca pearls (pages 186). Sweet Fermented Glutinous Rice (page 189) blurs the line between dessert and drink, while the Palm Sugar, Cashew and Coconut Parfait (pages 191) offers a modern take on Indonesian indulgence.

Together, these recipes reveal the breadth of Indonesia's sweet traditions – inventive, comforting and always full of character.

Spiced Coffee and Coconut Milk
Bajigur

Bajigur is a traditional Sundanese hot drink, typically enjoyed on cool days. Rich, comforting and a bit nostalgic, it's a sweet, spiced blend of coconut milk and palm sugar with warming aromatics – a hug in a cup. It has a bold, gingery coffee flavour but you can easily adjust the balance by reducing the ginger or adding more coffee to the brew.

Preparation time: 10 minutes
Cooking time: 10–15 minutes

Serves 4

* 50 g/1¾ oz fresh root ginger, finely grated
* 4 tablespoons freshly ground coffee
* 1 pandan leaf or 1 tablespoon vanilla extract
* 2½ tablespoons palm sugar or coconut sugar
* 200 ml/7 fl oz (scant 1 cup) coconut milk

Combine the ginger, coffee, pandan leaf and sugar in a pan. Pour in 300 ml/10 fl oz (1¼ cups) of water, then bring to the boil and simmer for 5–7 minutes.

Add the coconut milk, return to the boil and simmer for another 5 minutes.

Strain and serve hot.

Sour Turmeric Drink
Kunyit Asam Fermentasi

I once accidentally left a bottle of homemade *jamu kunyit* (turmeric drink) in the refrigerator for far too long and completely forgot about it. Four weeks later, expecting it to have gone off, I tentatively gave it a taste (curiosity got the better of me). To my surprise, it had transformed into a lightly fermented drink with a delicate sparkle. The flavour was still earthy from the turmeric but now mellowed, with a gentle tangy sweetness and subtle effervescence. What began as a mistake turned into a refreshing and unexpected discovery, proving that sometimes the best flavours come from happy accidents.

Preparation time: 15 minutes
Cooking time: 25 minutes

Makes 1.75 litres/60 fl oz (7½ cups)

* 70 g/2½ oz fresh turmeric
* 50 g/1¾ oz fresh root ginger
* 5 makrut lime leaves
* 1 stalk lemongrass, crushed and tied in a knot
* 1 pandan leaf, tied in a knot
* 180 g/6 oz palm sugar, coarsely chopped, or coconut sugar
* 120 g/4¼ oz tamarind pulp, torn into small pieces
* 1 teaspoon salt
* juice of 2 limes (optional)

Put the turmeric and ginger into a small blender and blend well.

Transfer the mixture to a large saucepan and add the remaining ingredients except the lime juice. Add 2 litres/68 fl oz (8½ cups) of water and bring to the boil, then reduce the heat to medium and simmer for 25 minutes, stirring occasionally.

Strain, then add the lime juice, if using, to give it sourness. Serve hot or at room temperature.

(Alternatively, it can be fermented at room temperature for up to 2 weeks [25°C/77°F] or 4 weeks in the refrigerator.)

Javanese Pandan-ginger Tonic
Sekoteng

Sekoteng is a warming drink-meets-dessert from Central Java, beloved for its ginger-spiced broth and surprising textures – toasted nuts, bread, mung beans and chewy tapioca pearls. Served piping hot, it's the perfect street-side treat for rainy evenings.

Preparation time: 30–40 minutes, plus 45 minutes soaking time
Cooking time: 45 minutes–1 hour

Serves 6–8

- 5 tablespoons sago pearls
- 50 g/1¾ oz (¼ cup) mung beans, soaked overnight, then drained
- 50 g/1¾ oz (scant ½ cup) blanched roasted peanuts
- 100 g/3½ oz fresh root ginger (remove any dry bits)
- 2 lemongrass stalks, crushed and tied into a knot
- 2 long pandan leaves, tied into a knot, or 1 tablespoon vanilla extract
- 100 g/3½ oz (scant ½ cup) coconut sugar
- 2 slices white or brown toast, cut into bite-size pieces
- coconut milk, for drizzling (optional)

Quickly rinse the sago pearls, then place them in a saucepan and cover with enough cold water to cover them by 5 cm (2 inches). Soak in cold water for 45 minutes.

Bring to the boil. Reduce heat to medium and simmer for 10 minutes, stirring occasionally, until the pearls turn translucent. Remove from the heat and drain into a bowl of cold water. Let sit for 5 minutes, then drain again. Transfer the pearls to a bowl, add 100 ml/3½ fl oz (scant ½ cup) of water. Set aside.

Meanwhile, bring a large saucepan of water to the boil. Add the mung beans and simmer over medium heat for 25 minutes, until the beans are tender but still intact. Strain, then set aside.

Char the ginger over a flame for 3 minutes, then add to a blender along with 800 ml/28 fl oz (3⅓ cups) of water. Blend well, then transfer to a pan.

Add the lemongrass, pandan leaves and the coconut sugar. Bring to the boil, then reduce the heat and simmer for 10 minutes. Strain, then return the mixture to the pan and keep warm.

To serve, divide the beans, peanuts and pandan-ginger broth among bowls. Add the tapioca pearls and the bread pieces and serve hot. If desired, drizzle 1–2 tablespoons of coconut milk over each bowl.

Cendol with Pandan Jelly and Coconut Milk
Es Cendol

Es cendol is a beloved iced dessert drink with vibrant green rice-flour jelly strands, coconut milk and palm sugar syrup. Refreshing, sweet and full of tropical nostalgia, it's perfect on a hot day.

Preparation time: 20 minutes
Cooking time: 25 minutes

Serves 4

- 6 pandan leaves, coarsely chopped
- 5 spinach leaves
- 2½ tablespoons cornflour (cornstarch)
- 2 tablespoons cassava or tapioca flour
- 60 g/3 ½ oz (½ cup) rice flour
- ½ teaspoon salt

For the sweet coconut milk:
- 400 ml/14 fl oz (1⅔ cups) coconut milk
- 1½ tablespoons sugar
- ½ pandan leaf, cut into 5-cm/2-inch pieces

For the palm sugar syrup:
- 200 g/7 oz (scant 1 cup) palm sugar or coconut sugar
- pinch of salt
- 4 ripe jackfruit pieces, cubed, or ½ pandan leaf, tied into a knot (optional)

In a blender, combine the pandan and spinach leaves. Pour in 500 ml/17 fl oz (generous 2 cups) and blend well. Strain through a fine-mesh sieve (strainer).

Pour the mixture into a saucepan. Add cornflour (cornstarch), both flours, salt and the pandan water. Simmer over medium heat for 10 minutes, until thickened and translucent.

Prepare a large bowl of iced water.

Press the warm green paste through a slotted spoon into the iced water to form jelly strands. Discard the iced water and transfer the strands to clean water. Use immediately.

To make the sweet coconut milk, combine all the ingredients in a saucepan with 100 ml/3½ fl oz (scant ½ cup) of water. Bring to the boil, then reduce the heat and simmer for 5 minutes. Leave to cool.

To make the palm sugar syrup, combine all the ingredients in a saucepan along with 3½ tablespoons of water. Simmer for 5 minutes, until the sugar is dissolved and the syrup is fragrant. Strain and leave to cool.

To serve, add 3–4 tablespoons of jelly strands to each glass. Pour 125 ml/4¼ fl oz (generous ½ cup) of the sweet coconut milk into each glass and drizzle with 2 tablespoons of the palm sugar syrup. Add crushed ice and enjoy.

Sweet Fermented Glutinous Rice

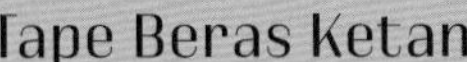

Tape Beras Ketan

I first came across *tape ketan* – a fermented sticky rice treat – in Ubud, Bali, through Ibu Ni Nyoman Sarianing, the aunt of chef Nyoman, who often helps out when I'm working in Indonesia. It's made by fermenting steamed glutinous rice with *ragi tape* (*Rhizopus oryzae*), a culture similar to wine yeast. Over time, the rice turns soft, sweet and slightly tangy and takes on a mild alcoholic aroma. Traditionally, it's tinted pale green with *katuk* leaves, but I've used spinach here just for the colour.

In Bali and Java, *tape ketan* is usually wrapped in banana leaves and eaten as a snack or served in chilled coconut milk drinks with tropical fruit. It also plays a role in ceremonial offerings, symbolizing prosperity and gratitude. The slow fermentation not only develops its unique flavour and texture but also speaks to the deep connection between food, ritual and tradition in Balinese and Javanese culture.

Preparation time: 20 minutes, plus 4 hours soaking time and 3–4 days fermentation
Cooking time: 30 minutes

Serves 6

- 500 g/1 lb 2 oz (2½ cups) glutinous rice, rinsed and soaked for 4 hours
- 10 large spinach leaves
- 10 g/¼ oz tapai yeast
- 2 tablespoons sugar
- fresh banana leaves

Drain the rice and rinse again. Place the rice in a steamer and steam for 15 minutes. (I use a bamboo steamer lined with baking [parchment] paper and spread the rice out in it.)

Meanwhile, combine the spinach and 175 ml/6 fl oz (¾ cup) of water in a blender. Blend and strain. It should yield 150 ml/5 fl oz (⅔ cup) of spinach water.

Place the rice in a bowl, then add the spinach water and mix well. Set aside for 10 minutes. The rice will absorb the liquid and turn light green.

Place the coloured rice in the steamer and steam for another 15 minutes. Transfer the rice to a tray and spread it around to cool down to room temperature.

Take a handful of rice in one hand and sprinkle with the yeast and sugar. Repeat until all the rice has been sprinkled with the yeast and sugar. (We do this to avoid disturbing the yeast too much.)

Line 2 containers with the banana leaves. Divide the rice into 4 portions and place into each container in a single layer. Top each container with more banana leaves. Place in a warm room (or near a warm radiator) and leave to ferment for 3–4 days, until the rice has a fruity aroma and a mildly alcoholic scent. It is ready to enjoy as is or in a dessert.

Palm Sugar, Cashew and Coconut Parfait

Es Krim Potong dengan Santan, Gula Aren dan Kacang Mede

Palm sugar, cashews and coconut milk are at the heart of many Indonesian desserts and create a perfect harmony of flavours when combined. The deep caramel notes of *gula aren*, with a subtle savoury edge, blend beautifully with the rich creaminess of coconut milk and the buttery crunch of cashews.

This summer treat is wonderfully easy to prepare and can be made well in advance. Unlike traditional frozen desserts, it doesn't require an ice-cream maker. Just pour the mixture into a mould, freeze for 12 hours and serve – no need to let it soften first. The texture is light, airy and smooth, much like a mousse but in sliceable form.

Preparation time: 30 minutes, plus 12 hours freezing time
Cooking time: 10 minutes

Serves 6–8

- 4 eggs, separated
- 2 tablespoons sugar
- 400 ml/14 fl oz (1⅔ cups) coconut milk
- 100 ml/3½ fl oz (scant ½ cup) Palm Sugar Syrup (page 188)
- 5 g/⅛ oz agar-agar
- 2 pandan leaves, tied into a knot, or 1 teaspoon vanilla extract
- 100 g/3½ oz (¾ cup) cashews, roasted and coarsely ground

Line a 900-g (2-lb) loaf pan with clingfilm (plastic wrap) and set aside.

Put the egg yolks in a heatproof bowl, add 1 tablespoon of the sugar and set over a saucepan of simmering water. Whisk with a whisk or hand-held blender until pale yellow, thick and doubled in volume. Remove from the pan and set aside to cool.

Combine the coconut milk, palm sugar syrup, agar-agar and pandan leaves in a saucepan. Mix well, then simmer for 6–8 minutes. Set aside to cool.

In a spotlessly clean bowl, whisk the egg whites until you have soft peaks. Add the remaining tablespoon of sugar and whisk until firm and glossy.

Fold half of the coconut milk mixture into the egg yolk mixture, then fold in the egg whites little by little until evenly combined.

Sprinkle the ground cashews over the base of the lined loaf pan, then pour in the egg yolk mixture. Drizzle over the remaining coconut mixture and use a chopstick to create a marbled effect with it. Freeze for at least 12 hours, until firm when pressed in the centre.

To serve, invert the loaf pan onto a flat serving dish and lift it off the parfait. Peel off the clingfilm and serve. Sprinkle with extra roasted ground cashew.

Chocolate Pudding with Vanilla Custard

Puding Coklat dengan Fla Vanila

This nostalgic Indonesian dessert takes me back to the Christmas parties of my childhood. Unlike Western chocolate puddings that use gelatine or cornflour (cornstarch), this version uses agar-agar, a plant-based gelling agent made from seaweed.

But what makes this dessert extra special is the *fla*, a classic Indonesian custard sauce made from milk, egg yolks, sugar and vanilla. While artificial vanilla was once the norm, today we're lucky to have easy access to fragrant, locally grown vanilla beans.

Preparation time: 20 minutes, plus 3 hours chilling time
Cooking time: 10–15 minutes

Serves 8

* 480 ml/16 fl oz (2 cups) full-fat (whole) milk
* 100 g/3½ oz (½ cup) sugar
* ½ teaspoon sea salt
* 180 g/6 oz dark chocolate
* 1 tablespoon agar-agar

For the custard:

* 250 ml/8 fl oz (1 cup) full-fat (whole) milk
* 75 g/2¾ oz (⅓ cup) sugar
* 1 vanilla bean or 1 tablespoon vanilla extract
* 8 egg yolks
* 200 ml/7 fl oz (scant 1 cup) single (light) cream

In a medium saucepan, combine 280 ml/9½ fl oz (1⅓ cups) of the milk with the sugar and salt and cook over medium heat for 4 minutes, until it starts to steam, whisking constantly to dissolve the sugar. Add the dark chocolate and cook for another 3 minutes, stirring occasionally, until the chocolate melts fully into the milk and the mixture is silky.

In a small bowl, whisk the remaining milk with the agar-agar. Pour into the chocolate milk, whisking constantly while bringing it to the boil over high heat, then turn the heat down to a gentle simmer and whisk constantly for 5 minutes.

Pour into any mould you desire. Carefully tap the mould a few times on the counter to release air bubbles. Chill in the refrigerator for 3 hours until completely set.

Meanwhile, make the custard. In a large bowl, combine the milk, sugar, vanilla and egg yolks. Mix well.

Strain the mixture through a fine-mesh sieve (strainer) into a medium saucepan and bring to a simmer over medium heat. Stir until thickened.

Remove the pan from the heat, then gradually whisk in the cream until combined. Set aside to cool, then refrigerate for at least 2 hours.

To serve, flip the pudding mould onto a clean counter or chopping (cutting) board and gently tap it a few times to release the pudding from the mould. Serve with the custard.

Blue Sago Pudding with Mango

Puding Sago Bunga Telang dan Mangga

This classic Indonesian sago pearl dessert gets a refreshing modern twist with a natural burst of colour and flavour. The pearls are tinted blue with *bunga telang* (butterfly pea flower), which grows abundantly across Indonesia, adding a striking hue without artificial colouring. To brighten the flavour, it's topped with a tangy coulis made from fresh, ripe strawberries – now widely cultivated by farmers in Java and Bali. Sweet mango, toasted almond flakes and a mix of seeds bring contrasting textures, creating a dessert that's as balanced as it is beautiful.

Preparation time:
25 minutes, plus 3 hours setting time
Cooking time: 25 minutes

Serves 4–6

For the strawberry jelly:
- 100 g/3½ oz strawberries, halved
- 300 ml/10 fl oz (1¼ cups) water
- 3 tablespoons sugar
- 1¼ teaspoons agar-agar

For the strawberry coulis:
- 150 g/5½ oz strawberries, trimmed and cut into bite-size cubes
- 2 tablespoons icing (confectioners') sugar
- ¼ teaspoon lime juice

For the pudding:
- 2 tablespoons dried butterfly pea flowers
- 100 g/3½ oz (⅔ cup) sago or cassava pearls
- 200 ml/7 fl oz (scant 1 cup) coconut milk
- 1 pandan leaf, tied into a knot, or 1 teaspoon vanilla extract
- 1 ripe mango, cut into 1-cm/½-inch cubes
- 20 g/¾ oz (¼ cup) almond flakes, toasted

First, make the strawberry jelly. Combine all the ingredients except the agar-agar in a blender and blend well. Strain through a fine-mesh sieve (strainer) into a saucepan, add the agar-agar and mix well. Bring to the boil over medium heat, then turn the heat off. Pour the mixture into a 13 x 20-cm/5 x 8-inch container. Set aside to cool, then refrigerate for 3 hours until set.

Next, make the strawberry coulis. Put all the ingredients into a pan. Bring to the boil, then reduce to a simmer for 10 minutes, until the strawberries are softened. Using a small blender, blend well and set aside.

Make the pudding. Put 600 ml/20 fl oz (2½ cups) of water into a saucepan and bring to the boil. Add the dried butterfly pea flowers and boil for 3–4 minutes. Strain the blue water into a bowl and set aside to cool. Add the sago pearls and soak for 30 minutes.

Bring the mixture to the boil, then reduce to a simmer. Cook for 10 minutes, until the sago pearls turn translucent and stir occasionally to prevent them from sticking together. Set aside for 3 minutes, until the sago pearls have turned blue. Drain, then transfer to a bowl of cold water. Refrigerate until needed.

In a saucepan, combine the coconut milk and pandan leaf. Bring to the boil, then set aside to cool. Refrigerate until needed.

To serve, cut the strawberry jelly into 1-cm/½-inch cubes. Put 3 tablespoons of sago pearls into serving bowls and top each with 2 tablespoons of strawberry jelly. Top each with mango cubes, 100 ml/3½ fl oz (scant ½ cup) of the flavoured coconut milk and 1–2 tablespoons of the strawberry coulis. Sprinkle with toasted almonds.

Coconut Pudding with Strawberries

Klappertaart dengan Stroberi

Klappertaart, a Dutch-Indonesian dessert from Manado, is another childhood favourite I grew up with. Traditionally, it's made with young coconut, custard, rum and spiced raisins, then baked to create a rich, custard-like pudding with a firm texture. In this version, I've chosen not to bake it, resulting in a lighter, more delicate pudding. I've also added fresh strawberries on top and finished it with a sprinkle of cinnamon. The result is surprisingly delicious – the sweet-tart strawberries balance the creamy richness of the coconut beautifully, while the warmth of cloves and cinnamon brings depth and a subtle spiced aroma that enhances the tropical flavours. The contrast of textures – soft coconut strands, juicy berries and silky custard – makes each bite even more enjoyable. This twist offers a refreshing yet comforting take on a beloved Manado dessert.

Preparation time: 25 minutes, plus 3 hours chilling time
Cooking time: 5 minutes

Serves 4–6

* 5 whole cloves
* 1 short cinnamon stick
* 100 g/3½ oz (⅔ cup) raisins
* 200 g/7 oz frozen young coconut meat, defrosted
* 50 g/1¾ oz (scant ½ cup) pili nuts or almond flakes, toasted
* 1 teaspoon ground cinnamon
* 100 g/3½ oz strawberries, sliced, to serve

For the vanilla custard:

* 6 egg yolks
* 100 g/3½ oz (½ cup) sugar
* 2 teaspoons cornflour (cornstarch)
* 250 ml/8 fl oz (1 cup) full-fat (whole) milk
* 1 vanilla bean, split and scraped
* 250 ml/8 fl oz (1 cup) double (heavy) cream
* 2 tablespoons dark rum

In a saucepan, combine 100 ml/3½ fl oz (scant ½ cup) of water, the cloves and cinnamon stick and bring to the boil. Add the raisins and simmer for 5 minutes, then drain, remove the cloves and cinnamon stick and leave to cool.

In a mixing bowl, beat the egg yolks, sugar and cornflour (cornstarch) for the custard until creamy.

Combine the milk, vanilla bean and seeds in a saucepan and heat gently until steaming. Slowly pour the hot milk into the egg mixture, stirring all the time until combined. Stir in the cream and the rum.

Pour the custard mixture back into the pan and stir over low heat until the mixture thickens sufficiently to coat the back of a wooden spoon. Remove the vanilla bean.

Divide the young coconut meat and raisins among 4–6 serving bowls or glasses and spoon the custard on top. Sprinkle with the pili nuts and ground cinnamon.

Put the glasses in the refrigerator and chill for at least 3 hours. Top with the sliced strawberries and serve.

Black Glutinous Rice Pudding with Palm Sugar and Mango

Bubur Ketan Hitam dengan Gula Aren dan Mangga

You'll find this dish across Indonesia, from street food stalls to family dining tables. At first glance, it may seem humble, but one spoonful is all it takes to realise how special it is. The soft, slightly chewy black glutinous rice pairs beautifully with the rich, caramel notes of *gula aren* (palm sugar), while slices of ripe mango add a bright, fruity contrast.

Serve it warm or chilled, with a swirl of coconut milk if you like, and let each bite take you somewhere sun-drenched and slow-paced.

Preparation time: 20 minutes, plus overnight soaking time
Cooking time: 45 minutes

Serves 10–12

* 250 g/9 oz (1¼ cups) black glutinous rice, rinsed and soaked overnight
* 125 g/4¼ oz (½ cup plus 2 tablespoons) white glutinous rice, rinsed and soaked overnight
* 2 pandan leaves, tied into a knot, or 20 g/¾ oz fresh root ginger, thinly sliced
* ½ teaspoon salt
* 3–4 ripe mangoes
* 250 ml/8 fl oz (1 cup) Palm Sugar Syrup (see page 188)
* 200 ml/7 fl oz (scant 1 cup) coconut milk
* 100 g/3½ oz (¾ cup) cashews, roasted and coarsely ground

Drain both types of rice. Rinse, then drain again.

Put both types of rice into a saucepan along with 1.5 litres/50 fl oz (6¼ cups) of water and the pandan leaves and salt. Bring to the boil, then simmer for 45 minutes, until the water has nearly evaporated. Remove from the heat and let sit at room temperature.

Peel and slice the mangoes.

To serve, put 3 tablespoons of rice into each bowl and top with 3 tablespoons of palm sugar syrup and 2 tablespoons of coconut milk. Sprinkle with ground roasted cashews and serve with the sliced mango on the side.

Lime Loaf with Sweet Kolak Sauce

Kue Bolu Jeruk Nipis dengan Saus Kolak Manis

V Ø

In Indonesia, we don't typically use lime in desserts – not even the zest – as it has a slightly bitter taste. But I wanted to try something different, and I found that when paired with sweet *kolak* sauce – a rich mixture of coconut sugar and coconut milk infused with pandan leaves – it creates a wonderful balance. The result is a refreshing cake that's perfect for afternoon tea or simply as a snack, reminiscent of iconic teatime treats in the UK.

My late mother-in-law used to make a lovely lemon drizzle cake, which inspired me to create this version – and take it a step further by making it a vegan-friendly treat using coconut oil and soy milk. The cake is beautifully moist, almost damp, with a rich, satisfying flavour. There's no need for cream, ice cream or any extras – just serve it as is, with a hot cup of tea.

Preparation time: 20 minutes
Cooking time: 30 minutes

Serves 8

* 120 g/4¼ oz (generous ⅔ cup) plain (all-purpose) flour
* 70 g/2½ oz (¾ cup) ground almonds
* 1 teaspoon bicarbonate of soda (baking soda)
* 1 teaspoon baking powder
* ¼ teaspoon salt
* zest of 4 limes, plus extra for garnish
* 100 g/3½ oz (½ cup) sugar
* 3½ tablespoons coconut oil or olive oil
* 3½ tablespoons lime juice
* 80 ml/2¾ fl oz (⅓ cup) soy milk
* 1 quantity Kolak Sauce (page 37)

Preheat the oven to 180°C/350°F/Gas Mark 4. Grease and line a 450-g (1-lb) loaf pan with baking (parchment) paper.

In a medium bowl, whisk the flour, ground almonds, bicarbonate of soda (baking soda), baking powder and salt. Set aside.

In a separate bowl, combine the lime zest and sugar. Using your fingertips, rub them together to release the oils and reduce the bitterness of the zest. Mix in the vanilla, the coconut oil, 1½ tablespoons of the lime juice and soy milk

Gradually add the flour mixture to the wet ingredients in 4 parts, whisking after each addition until well combined.

Pour the batter into the prepared loaf pan and bake for 30 minutes, until the loaf is golden and the top is set. A skewer inserted into the middle should come out clean. While the cake is still hot in the pan, drizzle over the remaining 2 tablespoons of lime juice. Allow the loaf to cool in the pan, then lift it out using the baking paper.

Place the loaf on a wire rack with a lipped baking sheet underneath to catch any drips. Garnish with lime zest. Drizzle generously with the kolak sauce – it won't set like frosting but adds richness. Add more sauce when serving.

The cake can be stored at room temperature in an airtight container for up to 3 days and the kolak sauce can be refrigerated for 5 days.

Banana and Pineapple Cake

Kue Pisang dan Nanas

Moist, warmly spiced and naturally sweet, this delicious cake brings tropical comfort to any table. Inspired by classic Indonesian flavours, it combines ripe bananas and juicy pineapple with cinnamon, vanilla and toasted nuts for texture. A tangy cream cheese frosting adds the perfect finish – rich, but balanced. It's an easy, crowd-pleasing bake that feels both familiar and just a little exotic.

Preparation time: 20 minutes
Cooking time: 30 minutes

Serves 12

For the cake:

* 300 g/10½ oz (2½ cups) plain (all-purpose) flour
* 1 teaspoon bicarbonate of soda (baking soda)
* pinch of salt
* 300 g/10½ oz (1½ cups) caster (superfine) sugar
* 300 ml/10 fl oz (1¼ cups) sunflower oil
* 2–3 bananas, mashed
* 3 eggs
* 1 tablespoon ground cinnamon
* 1 vanilla pod, seeds scraped
* 100 g/3½ oz (⅔ cup) finely chopped pineapple
* 100 g/3½ oz (¾ cup) roasted nuts, coarsely chopped, plus extra for garnish

For the frosting:

* 125 g/4½ oz (1 cup) icing (confectioners') sugar, sifted
* 100 g/3½ oz butter, at room temperature
* 250 g/8¾ oz (1 cup) cream cheese

Preheat the oven to 180°C/350°F/Gas Mark 4. Grease a baking pan.

In a large bowl, sift the flour, bicarbonate of soda (baking soda) and salt into a bowl. Set aside.

In a stand mixer fitted with the whisk attachment, combine the sugar, oil, mashed banana, eggs, cinnamon and vanilla seeds. Beat until smooth and well combined. Gradually add the flour mixture, beating gently until just incorporated. Fold in the diced pineapple and chopped nuts.

Pour the batter into the prepared pan and smooth the surface with a spatula. Bake for 30 minutes, until golden brown and a skewer inserted into the centre comes out clean. Allow the cake to cool slightly in the pan, then transfer to a wire rack to cool completely.

To make the frosting, combine the butter and icing (confectioners') sugar in a large bowl. Using a handheld mixer, mix on medium speed until smooth. Add the cream cheese and beat for 2 minutes, until light and creamy.

Spread the frosting evenly over the cake. Sprinkle with reserved nuts and a little cinnamon if desired. Serve.

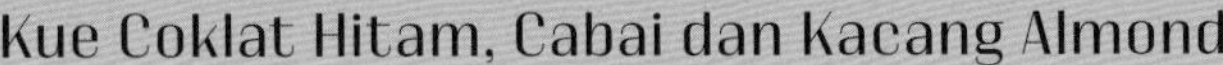

Dark Chocolate, Chilli and Almond Cake

Kue Coklat Hitam, Cabai dan Kacang Almond

Chocolate and chilli are long-time partners in flavour, and here, they shine alongside a nutty, tender almond cake that ties everything together. The soft crumb provides balance, comfort and texture, rounding out the boldness of the chocolate and spice.

This dessert is more than just a sweet treat – it's a nod to Indonesia's cacao heritage. It also honours traditional methods and regional ingredients, featuring a subtle touch of plant-based smoked salt from Papua, which adds depth and complexity to every bite.

Preparation time: 20 minutes
Cooking time: 35–40 minutes

Serves 10

- 225 g/8 oz butter, at room temperature, plus extra for greasing
- 250 g/9 oz best-quality dark chocolate (70% cocoa solids), chopped
- 2 tablespoons strong coffee
- 200 g/7 oz (1 cup) caster (superfine) sugar
- 6 eggs, separated
- 2 tablespoons icing (confectioners') sugar, plus extra for dusting
- 1 tablespoon chilli powder
- 200 g/7 oz (2 cups) ground almonds

Preheat the oven to 160°C/325°F/Gas Mark 3. Grease a 28-cm/11-inch cake pan with butter and line with baking (parchment) paper.

Melt the chocolate and coffee in a heatproof bowl set over a saucepan of simmering water, ensuring the base of the bowl does not touch the water. Stir in the butter and caster (superfine) sugar, until all the sugar has dissolved. Remove from the heat.

In a separate, spotlessly clean bowl, beat the egg whites and icing (confectioners') sugar until firm. Set aside.

In a separate bowl, lightly beat the egg yolks, then stir into the chocolate mixture. Mix in the chilli powder and ground almonds. Add a spoonful of the beaten egg whites and fold in. Continue adding the egg whites in the same way until fully incorporated.

Transfer the mixture to the prepared pan and bake for 35 minutes, until slightly gooey in the centre. Cool completely in the pan.

Transfer to a serving plate. The cake develops a thin, crusty layer on the outside when it cools. Dust with icing sugar.

Manado-style Coconut Macarons
Kue Kelapa

Coconut macarons are a beloved traditional treat from Manado, North Sulawesi – where coconuts are abundant and deeply woven into the region's culinary heritage. This simple yet satisfying confection is made from freshly grated coconut, egg whites and sugar, resulting in a chewy texture with a crisp, golden exterior.

Unlike the refined French macarons, ours are rustic – often shaped into half-moons and baked until lightly browned. In Manado, I would occasionally add pili nuts (often called the local almond), but here, I've replaced them with ground almonds for convenience.

Whether enjoyed as an afternoon snack or served during festive occasions, they capture the essence of Manado's rich tradition of coconut-based sweets.

Preparation time: 10 minutes
Cooking time: 15 minutes

Makes around 14–16

* 3 egg whites
* ¼ teaspoon cream of tartar
* 100 g/3½ oz (scant ¾ cup) icing (confectioners') sugar
* 50 g/1¾ oz (½ cup) ground almonds
* ½ teaspoon salt
* seeds of 1 vanilla bean or 1 teaspoon vanilla extract
* scant 2 tablespoons caster (superfine) sugar
* 125 g/4¼ oz (1½ cups) unsweetened desiccated coconut

Preheat the oven to 170°C/338°F/Gas Mark 3 for 5 minutes, then reduce the temperature to 160°C/325°F. Line a baking sheet with baking (parchment) paper.

In a spotlessly clean bowl, beat the egg whites for 45 seconds, or until frothy. Add the cream of tartar, then gradually add the icing (confectioners') sugar. Beat until soft peaks form.

Fold in the ground almonds, salt, vanilla, caster (superfine) sugar and coconut. The mixture will be sticky but should hold its shape.

Using two spoons, form the mixture into small, round dome shapes on the prepared baking sheet, spacing them apart. Bake for 12 minutes, or until golden brown. Remove from the oven and leave to cool for 5 minutes. Gently remove each of the coconut macarons to a wire rack.

The coconut macarons can be stored in an airtight container at room temperature for up to 3 days.

Mung Bean Porridge
Bubur Kacang Ijo

Few dishes evoke warmth and nostalgia quite like *bubur kacang ijo* – a humble yet deeply comforting Indonesian porridge made from mung beans, palm sugar and coconut milk, gently infused with pandan or ginger. Slow-cooked until the beans are tender and creamy, this porridge carries a natural sweetness that soothes and nourishes.

My Italian friend, an art restorer based in Jakarta, adores this dish – and I understand why. Whether served warm on a rainy afternoon or chilled as a refreshing treat, this dish wraps you in a sense of comfort. It's traditionally served at breakfast but it also works as a delicious dessert.

Preparation time: 5 minutes, plus overnight soaking time
Cooking time: 40 minutes

Serves 6–8

- 300 g/10½ oz mung beans, rinsed and soaked overnight
- 2 long pandan leaves, tied into a knot, or 20 g/¾ oz fresh root ginger, thinly sliced
- 1 teaspoon salt

To serve:
- 400 ml/14 fl oz (1⅔ cups) coconut milk
- 100 ml/3½ fl oz (scant ½ cup) Palm Sugar Syrup (page 188)

Discard any floating mung beans from their soaking bowl, then drain.

In a saucepan, combine the beans, pandan leaves and salt. Add 750 ml/25 fl oz (3 cups) of water and boil for 40 minutes, until the mung beans are very tender.

Serve warm or at room temperature. Add the coconut milk and palm sugar syrup to the beans. (I like to put the coconut milk and palm sugar syrup in separate jugs for guest to serve themselves.)

As a rough guide, I add 1 ladleful of mung beans and water to a small bowl, then add 2 tablespoons of coconut milk and 1–2 tablespoons of palm sugar syrup.

Variation:
- **Mung Bean and Coconut Ice Cream**
  Blend the soft mung beans along with the water, coconut milk and palm sugar syrup in a blender, then transfer to an ice cream maker and churn according to the manufacturer's instructions.

Baked Cheesecake with Fermented Cassava

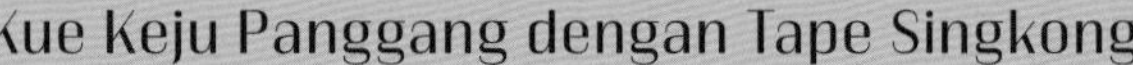

Kue Keju Panggang dengan Tape Singkong

This isn't a classic Indonesian dessert, but a modern fusion inspired by Basque cheesecake. It celebrates the marriage of a humble traditional ingredient – fermented cassava – with contemporary technique. The cassava's natural tang and earthiness beautifully complement the rich, creamy texture of the cheesecake, creating a unique balance of old and new. This cake not only elevates cassava but also reflects the spirit of blending tradition with innovation – a delicious tribute to local ingredients reimagined in a modern pudding.

Preparation time: 15 minutes, plus 4 hours chilling time
Baking time: 50–55 minutes

Serves 10

* butter, for greasing
* 300 g/10½ oz Fermented Cassava (page 45), mashed
* 560 g/20 oz (2 cups) cream cheese, at room temperature
* 200 g/7 oz (1 cup) mascarpone cheese, at room temperature
* 200 g/7 oz (1 cup) sugar
* 5 eggs
* 1 tablespoon vanilla extract
* 1 tablespoon plain (all-purpose) flour (optional)

Preheat the oven to 200°C/400°F/Gas Mark 6. Grease a 23-cm (9-inch) springform pan with butter and line the bottom and sides with baking (parchment) paper, making sure the paper extends above the rim to allow for the cake's rise.

Remove the fermented cassava stalks, then place it in a large mixing bowl and mash it with a fork.

In a separate bowl, combine the cream cheese, mascarpone and sugar. Whisk until smooth and creamy. Add the eggs, one at a time, whisking well after each addition, and mix until the batter is smooth. Using a rubber spatula, fold in the mashed fermented cassava. For a slightly firmer texture, add 1 tablespoon of flour. Mix well.

Pour the batter into the prepared cake pan and smooth the top with the spatula. Bake for 50–55 minutes, until the top is golden brown and slightly cracked and the centre jiggles a bit when you shake the pan.

Set aside to cool completely, then refrigerate for at least 4 hours, preferably overnight, to set.

Carefully remove the cheesecake from the springform pan and serve chilled.

Index

Page numbers in *italics indicate photos.*

Recipe Notes

Unless otherwise specified:

- Butter is unsalted.
- All spices are freshly ground.
- Eggs and individual vegetables and fruits, such as carrots and apples, are assumed to be medium-sized.
- All sugar is white caster (superfine) sugar and all brown sugar is cane or demerara (turbinado).
- All cream is 36–40% fat whipping (heavy) cream.
- All milk is full-fat (whole) at 3% fat, homogenised and lightly pasteurised.
- All salt is kosher salt.
- Parsley is flat-leaf (Italian).
- Breadcrumbs are always dried.
- All fresh root spices, such as ginger, turmeric and galangal, are left unpeeled, but you should trim off any old parts.
- Use vegetarian miso paste, as some varieties contain bonito (fish flakes).

Cooking times are for guidance only, as individual ovens vary. If using a conventional oven, follow the manufacturer's instructions concerning oven temperatures.

Exercise a high level of caution when following recipes involving any potentially hazardous activity, including the use of high temperatures and open flames and when deep-frying. In particular, when deep-frying, add food carefully to avoid splashing, wear long sleeves and never leave the pan unattended.

Some recipes include raw or very lightly cooked eggs and fermented products. These should be avoided by the elderly, infants, pregnant people, convalescents and anyone with an impaired immune system.

Because some species of mushrooms have been known to cause allergic reactions and illness, do take extra care when cooking and eating mushrooms, and do seek immediate medical help if you experience a reaction after preparing or eating them.

Exercise caution when making fermented products, ensuring all equipment is spotlessly clean, and seek expert advice if in any doubt.

When no quantity is specified, for example of oils used for finishing dishes or for deep-frying, quantities are discretionary and flexible.

All herbs, shoots, flowers and leaves should be picked fresh from a clean source. Exercise caution when foraging for ingredients; any foraged ingredients should be eaten only if an expert has deemed them safe to eat.

Both metric and imperial measures are used in this book. Follow one set of measurements throughout, not a mixture, as they are not interchangeable.

All spoon and cup measurements are level, unless otherwise stated. 1 teaspoon = 5 ml; 1 tablespoon = 15 ml. Australian standard tablespoons are 20 ml, so Australian readers are advised to use 3 teaspoons in place of 1 tablespoon when measuring small quantities.

Phaidon Press Limited
2 Cooperage Yard
London E15 2QR

Phaidon Press Inc.
111 Broadway
New York, NY 10006

Phaidon SARL
55, rue Traversière
75012 Paris

phaidon.com

First published 2026

ISBN 978 1 83729 111 3

A CIP catalogue record for this book is available from the British Library and the Library of Congress.

Commissioning Editor: Emilia Terragni
Project Editor: Michelle Meade
Production Controller: Gary Hayes
Design: Hans Stofregen
Layouts: Cantina
Photography: Yuki Sugiura

Additional photography on pages 4, 6, 30, 46, 96, 116, 138 and 221–222 courtesy of Petty Pandean-Elliott.

Printed in China

Publisher's Acknowledgements
Phaidon would like to thank James Brown, Adela Cory, Alex Jorge, Marnie Lamb, Laura Lawrence, João Mota, Aya Nishimura, Emily Preece-Morrison, Faye Robinson, Ellie Smith, Tracey Smith and Ana Teodoro.

Author's Acknowledgements
My deepest thanks to my family for their love and to friends and colleagues for their support. Thank you to Dumasi Samosir Wongso, Helianti Hilman, Ayu Kresna, Bli Gede Kresna and Switi Nyoman for sharing their culinary traditions; to Yuki Sugiura, Laura Lawrence, Alex Jorge, Aya Nishimura and Rene Viner for their artistry. Special thanks to Emilia Terragni, Michelle Meade and the Phaidon team for their guidance and to readers for embracing this book and the rich traditions of Indonesian food.